WANDERING IN CUBA
REVOLUTION AND BEYOND

Other Wanderland Writers Anthologies

2010 *Wandering in Costa Rica: Landscapes Lost and Found*

2012 *Wandering in Bali: A Tropical Paradise Discovered*

2013 *Wandering in Paris: Luminaries and Love in the City of Light* (First Place, London Book Festival Awards; Honorable Mention, Paris Book Festival Awards)

2015 *Wandering in Cornwall: Mystery, Mirth and Transformation in the Land of Ancient Celts* (IndieFab Winner, Foreword's Book of the Year Awards; Finalist, New Generation Indie Book Awards; Honorable Mention, London Book Festival Awards; Honorable Mention, Paris Book Festival Awards)

2016 *Wandering in Andalusia: The Soul of Southern Spain*

WANDERING IN CUBA
REVOLUTION AND BEYOND

Edited by
Linda Watanabe McFerrin and
Joanna Biggar

Wanderland Writers
Oakland, California

Copyright © 2018 Wanderland Writers. All rights reserved.
No part of this publication may be reproduced, distributed, or transmitted in any form or by any means, including photocopying, recording, or other electronic or mechanical methods, without the prior written permission of the publisher, except in the case of brief quotations embodied in critical reviews and certain other noncommercial uses permitted by copyright law.

For permission to print essays in this volume, grateful acknowledgement is made to the holders of copyright named on pages 213-223.

The lyrics on pages 21 and 23 are by songwriters Frank Loesser / Victor Schertzinger. "Sand In My Shoes" lyrics © Sony/ATV Music Publishing LLC.

The translation on page 79 is from *Dust Disappears, Poems by Carilda Oliver Labra*, translated by Daniela Gioseffi with a Foreword by Gregory Rabassa, Cross-Cultural Communications: Merrick, NY, Copyright ©1995 by Daniela Gioseffi. Reprinted by permission of the translator.

The poem on page 199, "VII," is reprinted with permission from the publisher of "Versos sencillos/Simple Verses" by Jose Marti (©1997 Arte Público Press - University of Houston).

Photographs:
Front cover, © Laurie McAndish King; back cover cityscape © Laurie McAndish King; back cover editor photo © Adrienne Amundsen
Interior photos: pages viii, xviii, 12, 20, 30, 38, 48, 52, 92, 100, 110, 198, 210, 212 © Laurie McAndish King; pages 4, 154 © Anne Woods; pages 62, 124, 164, 192 © Tania Amochaev; pages 66, 118 © Sandra Bracken; pages 84, 208 © Linda Watanabe McFerrin; page 138 © Douglas Hale; page 146 © Linda Jue; page 172 © Robert Markowitz; pages 74, 182 images from Wikimedia Commons; page 132 © Liborio Noval

Cover design, interior design and map by Jim Shubin,
www.bookalchemist.net
Typefaces: Sabon and Garamond

CATALOGING DATA:
Wandering in Cuba: Revolution and Beyond
Edited by Linda Watanabe McFerrin and Joanna Biggar

ISBN: 978-1-7327747-3-5
First printing 2018
Printed in the United States of America

"Hemingway, Cuba, and Me" won first place in the 2018 contest sponsored by America's leading travel writing conference, the Book Passage Travel Writers and Photographers Conference.

"Landing in Cuba" is a finalist in the 2018 William Wisdom-William Faulkner Creative Writing Competition, one of America's leading literary competitions.

Special thanks to Educational Adventures and their Cuban partner, Locally Sourced, for their guidance in creating and delivering on a wonderful Cuban experience.

For Thanasis Maskaleris—poet, scholar, fellow traveler, literary guide and beloved friend—who could not join us on this journey, and for the poets and artists of Cuba, whom he would have embraced.

Fidel poster at the entrance to a small museum

Contents

Introduction	xii
Foreword, Jeff Greenwald	xiv
"I Will Not Be Accompanying You to Cuba," Joanna Biggar	1
Landing in Cuba, Anne Woods	5
The Color of Words, Cyndi Goddard	13
My Havana Hallucination, Robert Markowitz	21
Cuba Through the Looking Glass, Laurie McAndish King	31
True Blood, Adrienne Amundsen	39
Falling for Havana, Christine Berardo	49
Hemingway, Cuba and Me, Anne Sigmon	53
Moments of Havana, MJ Pramik	63
An Old Woman and the Sea, Sandra Bracken	67
The Poet, the Poems, the Map, and Matanzas, Joanna Biggar	75
Deliberating on Che, Linda Watanabe McFerrin	85
My First Time, Tom Harrell	93
Cuba—Full of Flavor, Laurie McAndish King	101

Behind Closed Doors, Christine Berardo	111
My Malecón, Sandra Bracken	119
Behind the Façade, Tania Amochaev	125
Another Kind of Hero, Donna Hemmila	133
¿Viva la Revolucion?, Douglas Hale	139
Being *Nadie*, Linda Jue	147
Cuba: It's Complicated, MJ Pramik	155
Finding My Coda, Carol J. Kelly	165
¡Bailemos!, Donna Hemmila	173
At the Crack of the Bat, MJ Pramik	183
Camagüey with Me, Tania Amochaev	193
Haunted Havana, Jonathan Taylor	199
Poet, for Thanasis, Linda Watanabe McFerrin	209
Glossary	211
Contributor Bios	213
Editor Bios	222

CUBA

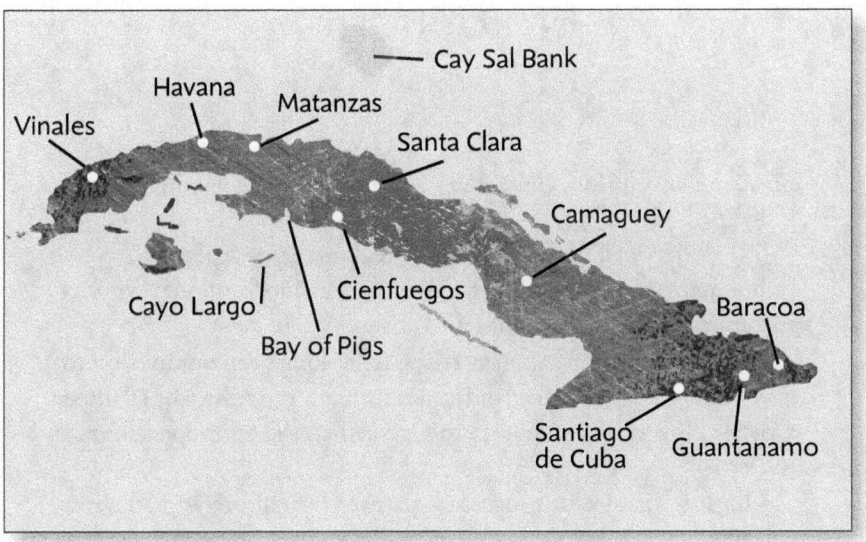

Introduction

Since the Revolution, Cuba, our close Caribbean neighbor, has been sadly inaccessible.

The doors open, the doors close, the doors open again.

For many North Americans, Cuba has remained a mystery, viewed in a mirror clouded by rumor and crisis.

As editors of the *Wandering* series, it has long been our mission to shed light on provocative landscapes through the stories of talented writers. How could we not go to Cuba when the door opened once more?

Our first visit yielded surprises, parts of the culture we had never imagined.

Our second visit, with two different groups of writers, revealed a kaleidoscope of art, culture, politics and ideas. What shocked us were the changes. We were witnessing a culture in transition, a country where entrepreneurial spirit was ignited and creativity in full force.

This was not the grey communist state of past decades. Vital, youthful, hope and spirit-filled, Cuba revealed the delightful, unquenchable passion and vigor that have allowed it to survive many hardships.

Introduction

Wander with us from city to countryside, enjoying the history, the rhythms, the tastes, the sights, and the soul of this amazing island. Everywhere, of course, we encountered its Revolution and recorded our understanding of its triumphs and failures. But we also experienced Cuba in its present reality, beyond the Revolution. Sometimes dark, sometimes salacious, sometimes funny, inspiring and warm, these stories will give you a sense of what happens when the walls come down.

—Linda Watanabe McFerrin and Joanna Biggar
 Oakland, California

Foreword

For years, the very idea of Cuba intimidated me. It was one of those flashpoint countries, like Israel or Tibet, of which all my knowledge was second hand and alarmist. When I thought of Cuba, I thought of course of Castro; of revolution; of desperate food shortages, empty stores; and a repressed population gazing bitterly north, across the 90-odd miles that separated so many of the island's people from their families and fortunes.

But the reality of my four journeys to Cuba—in the Spring months of 2011, 2012, 2013 and 2014—was a total contrast to my catastrophizing imagination. Cuba was wonderful. It was culturally rich and geographically fascinating, with as warm and welcoming a vibe as any place I'd visited in my 35 years as a travel journalist. In my overlapping memories of those visits, the country glows in a series of short vignettes: episodes from each of my trips tumbling together like gems in a funky kaleidoscope.

I can't summarize Cuba's history or culture or present-day aspirations for you. I'm not qualified to do so. But I can recall a few moments that, among hundreds of others, showed me that Cuba, with all its complexities and contradictions, is a place to admire:

Foreword — Jeff Greenwald

a country that seems to be having the time of its life, and invites you to join right in.

—Driving back to Havana from the coastal town of Matanzas, the Atlantic gleaming to the north, our little tour van pulls into a small gas station. While our driver fills the tank, we wander over to the attached open-air bar that only sells piña coladas. For a few pesos, I am handed a half-full glass of cold pineapple-coconut juice. On the bar stand two bottles of Havana Club, which flows like water in this rum-soaked country. I mix my own drink (refills free) as the grinning bargirl in braces practices her maracas for an upcoming concert. It doesn't hit me until we're driving away: *a bar at a gas station.* ¡Dios Mio!

—On the Malecón in Havana, 1 a.m. on a Saturday morning. T-shirt warm. Stars hazy through the sea mist, the sound of old guitars, families leaning against the stone breakwater singing and laughing, children chasing each other with water guns. I stop to gaze out at the ocean. A few yards down from me, a group of half a dozen young teenagers, visiting Havana for a nationwide competition, begin practicing their ballet moves. They perch on their pointes, lift their legs straight above their heads, leap in grande jetés as seagulls circle above them. They gleefully shake my hand then melt away, arms around each others' shoulders.

—One Spring afternoon my mother, an artist, sits sketching on a bench in the Plaza des Armas: a tree-lined square filled with open-air stalls selling antiquarian books. A woman with long dark hair and floral print dress walks up and shyly asks if she might borrow Mom's sketchbook and pencils. She slips in beside us, and in moments dashes off a magical drawing of a man with leaves, branches, and flocks of birds emerging from the crown of his head. She hands the pad back with a smile—casually mentioning that she currently has a one-woman show in the museum just behind us.

Life in Cuba is lived on a human scale. Interactions are person to person. You are drawn in, included, questioned, respected, teased, flirted with, asked to share art and music, cigars and rum, the honesty of your smile, the pesos in your purse. It's disarming and fabulous and fair.

Is Cuba perfect? Of course not. My point of view as an American traveler is, of course, shallow. Though the country is changing rapidly, it is a very different thing to visit than it is to live there. I'll never have to apply for a driver's license in Cuba, or thread the bureaucracy for a building permit. I'll never long for an iPhone I can't afford, be denied a passport, or stare over the Gulf of Mexico and wonder when I'll see my aunt again.

Fidel Castro is gone now, and Cuba is on the brink of ... well, something. But if the country has one thing that is indelible, it is a profound sense of community. That spirit is obvious when you drive through the litter-free towns, go to a baseball game, or ask locals what they think of the changes exploding across their island. For while most of them welcome the opportunity to own homes and create businesses, they also insist that their fellow countrymen benefit from Cuba's socialist legacy: universal health care, free education, daycare for working parents.

I don't know where the future is leading Cuba. During my first visit in 2011, it was described as a place "where anything is possible, and everything is impossible." Today, it is a place where anything really is possible. I hope that, as you read the stories in this collection, a sense of that infinite potential inspires you to make that very short flight to our very misunderstood neighbor. You'll find nothing intimidating (except, maybe, some of the salsa dancers) and much that is pure magic.

—Jeff Greenwald
Author of *The Size of the World* and *Snake Lake*

You would be traveling elsewhere ...

"I Will Not Be Accompanying You to Cuba"

Joanna Biggar

Remembering Thanasis, December 2017

Thanasis, I looked for
the poem in the words
as you spoke them.
I knew,
did not want to know,
what you were saying.

You would be traveling elsewhere.

So quickly you flew from us,
you left me grounded.
To find you,
to say good-bye
I walked your sacred lake
Temescal

Wandering in Cuba

looking for the wave of
your white hair in the wind,
your smile, your joke.
I found only the stillness of fishermen,
babies asleep like kings,
children skipping stones;
heard the nannies' laughter,
the runners' footfalls,
the seabird's cry.

There among your oaks and acorns,
your rocks and redwoods,
in the secret places
beyond the tall reeds,
in the earth cracks
where you met
beloved souls who had gone before,
I searched
but could not find you.

Then the crow lifted its wings above the lake,
calling out my lament
black and rippling like the water below,
a sob, a joke, a poem.

Now I am flying to Cuba.

Havana from the air

LANDING IN CUBA
Anne Woods

From the air, Cuba looks like any other island at this latitude—its green footprint, rim of white sand, pale aqua bleeding into the black-blue of the Gulf Stream current. My flight descends and the cabin warms. The 737 breathes in humid Caribbean air. I had long pictured Cuba in the reverse, its geography framed by a departure, rather than arrival. Many times I had heard the story of a family we knew who escaped in their small airplane in 1960, months after the Revolution. "Look at our land," the man said to his wife. "God only knows when we'll see it again." Their last view of Cuba had been of it receding, dipping over the horizon, disappearing forever.

Their departure was hot, convective, filled with regret. I trace their route in reverse, eager to see this, until recently, forbidden place. It is a small glimpse into their world—a world in which this new 737 I step off of seems eerily out of place.

In Havana, history presses in upon you. In January 1928, a new airline, Pan American Airways, flew its first passenger route, from Key West, Florida, to Havana. The ninety-mile flight cost $100 round-trip. In the United States, movies were no longer silent and the country was in its eighth year of Prohibition. In Cuba they were dancing the rumba and rum flowed. Wealthy Americans eager for a drink flocked to Havana. That year, Ernest Hemingway would visit Havana for the first time and fall in love with this sliver of Europe in the New World.

An hour after bouncing down the dirt runway in Key West, Pan American's Fokker F-VIII trimotor, named the *General Machado*, after Cuba's president, descended. Morning sun laved Havana in warmth. At its north edge was the half-moon of the seawall along the Malecón's promenade. The coast cleaved where the Bay of Havana fingered in along the old Spanish city. This part of the city, founded in 1519, was veined with narrow streets, and Havana spread out from it, its avenues broad and palm-lined. It was called the "Paris of the Caribbean," and even from above, Havana looked exotic—its buildings in the Spanish colonial, baroque and neoclassical styles. American influences were already visible in Havana's newly constructed Art Deco buildings.

Cuba's days of excess ended abruptly. The severity of change shocked even Abel Hera Corton, a Cuban pilot who had, in the months leading up to the Revolution, aided Fidel Castro and his rebel forces as they hid in the Sierra Maestra mountains, plotting to overthrow U.S.-backed dictator Fulgencio Batista.

By profession, Hera ran a crop dusting business, but he longed for change in Cuba. He began flying supplies to Castro and his men. Wealthy Cubans, whose trust in Batista had faded, gave cash, generators, wires, medicine and other necessities to Hera to deliver. Castro, then a thirty-two year old with a law degree, and Hera, thirty-four years old, talked of plans for what would come after the Revolution succeeded.

On January 1, 1959, Batista abdicated. Castro appointed Hera a major in the Rebel Army and put him in charge of agricultural aviation in Cuba. Hera quickly grew disenchanted with Castro's leftist leanings. Word of his dissention spread. In the months following the Revolution, private aircraft, like Hera's, were seized, and civilian pilots began to be executed for "counterrevolutionary activities." A warrant was issued for Hera's arrest.

The sun rose hot over the Vazquez airport in Ciego de Avila in the eastern province of Camagüey on May 19, 1960. The previous day, Hera had purchased a 1957 Cessna 182A. Inside the Cessna, his wife, Gladys, and their two small children, Abel and Mable, waited in the growing heat. Hera had filed a flight plan to Santa Fe airport in Havana, where he told an old friend at the airport, he was taking the children to enroll them in school. The two men agreed to meet later that evening for dinner.

The cabin cooled as they climbed. Hera circled around to a westerly heading, toward Havana. Below, two military vehicles sped toward the airport. They carried soldiers armed with machine guns. If they had delayed their takeoff, he told his wife, "I would be a prisoner and you on your way to become [sic] a widow right now."

Hera continued west over Las Villas, then banked the Cessna north. The Hera family watched the last of their world fall away behind them. Ahead was the deep cleft of water separating Cuba and the United States. Over Cay Sal, Hera made a position report to Havana Control. He said he estimated Havana in forty-five minutes. The controller ordered him to report when over Boyeros, Havana's main airport. Hera's reply was short: "Negative, Havana Control, I am within sight of the Florida Keys. Cuba shall be free!"

For a map, Hera carried the torn-out page of a geography book. He tuned the Cessna's ADF to an English-language radio station in Ft. Lauderdale, Florida, and homed in on the signal. Hera didn't speak English, but he knew the sound of freedom.

Eventually, Hera found his way back to aviation and replaced one of the airplanes he'd left behind in Cuba, a 1937 Stinson Reliant. Years later, he would sell the Stinson to my husband and his father. Hera was eighty-one by then, living on an airport outside Miami. His truck had a bumper sticker that read: "John Wayne, a true American hero!" There was a Jack Russell named Freedom. "Freedom. Come here, girl," someone called as the dog sped about. Hera's son, Abel, pointed to the Cessna 182, tucked away in a hangar. "This is the airplane we escaped in," he said.

In Havana, I had landed in the Hera family's world—a place of midcentury-American cars and old appliances. In many ways, Cuba hasn't changed in the fifty-eight years since they left. Somewhere on the island, the car they drove to the airport the day of their escape is likely still on the road. Here, the past is everywhere: in cracked facades, crumbling buildings that were once grand, colors muted and greyed. The city balances between two worlds, at once frozen and vibrant.

Havana, as she did before the Revolution, once again lusts after tourists. Four million of them visited Cuba in 2017. Street hustlers work the sidewalks. "Good to see you again," they say. "Taxi?" They push knock-off cigars rolled from banana leaves or paper. School children tear up their textbooks and sell origami flowers folded from their pages. As if in anticipation of tourists' questions, some restaurants and businesses have a poster or plaque that reads: *"Aqui jamas estuvo Hemingway."* Hemingway was not here.

One morning, Odette, the host of my *casa particular*, apologizes in Spanish as she sets small packets of margarine out with breakfast. There is a butter shortage. Sometimes when a cruise ship provisions, she explains, it cleans the city out of staples.

In nightclubs, Havana's twenty- and thirty-something year olds dress in styles chic enough to pass them off as New Yorkers, down to their iWatches. A newly moneyed class is rising up in Cuba, most of them working in the tourist industry.

With the influx of capital from tourism, buildings slowly perfuse with color: bright aquas, lime greens, yellows, pinks, the palest of blues. Street carts dwarf under bundles of pink and white gladiolus flowers, red roses, tubs of spearmint. Long braids of garlic and red onions dangle over their sides. 1950s-era Buicks, Chevrolets, Chryslers and Oldsmobiles taxi tourists, the cars' bodies thick with paint to stave off the corrosive tropical air.

A hot pink sedan of 1980s Russian vintage zooms by a dilapidated multi-rise. Laundry flaps above sidewalks. Caged parakeets chirp. A black rooster crows from a second-story balcony. One evening "Endless Love" blares through the courtyard of our *casa particular*, then the humid air quiets again. Over the din of occasional Spanish words, a dog barks. Later, the little dog, Kuku, greets us in the parlor, wearing a baby's long-sleeved shirt. It is nearly Christmas, and Havana's evening temperature has dipped into the high 60s.

Water pools among uneven cobblestones on streets wet from afternoon rain. Even after the rain stops, the standing water persists. "Old pipes," our guide, Yoli, says. "This is why we have dengue fever and Zika. Well, more dengue."

The air is thick with the odor of natural gas and garbage, the latter mounded on narrow sidewalks and spilling into streets. Cats gorge themselves on spoiled food from ripped-open bags. I don't have to see the place at night to know Havana teems with rats.

Often, there is the reek of decaying flesh. Once it is from three black goat legs severed cleanly at the knee, their silken fur gleaming in dim streetlight. A few days later, it is from the rear quarter of a white goat. At other places, I see chicken feet. These are offerings to the spirits of Santería, the Afro-Caribbean religion that came to Cuba with the slave trade.

At night, music drifts through Old Havana. A cat slinks through a cracked door near an old woman who sits in a plastic chair in her doorway. On the other side of a screen, a family watches television from their couch, dinner plates on their laps.

One evening at 10 p.m. Yoli takes us to a nightclub and art gallery, La Fábrica de Arte Cubano, that has been carved out of a former peanut oil factory. There is a portrait of a man with an exceptionally poetic name, Don Juan Domingo de La Fuente Castilliano, and a photograph of a sixty-something couple sitting on their bed in their underwear. The man is lighting a cigarette and his wife is staring straight into the camera, unsmiling, her breasts sagging across her stomach. "Sex Machine" blasts from the dance floor below.

On our return, we ride in an ancient taxi that smells of gasoline and doesn't have seat belts. The motor stalls at an intersection, and the driver cranks the engine over again. Dropping us at our *casa particular*, the Bond-o and rattle-can-red contraption speeds away, a black nimbus of exhaust following in its wake. At the end of each day in Havana, this is what I smell, in my hair and on my clothes. It is the sooty, incomplete combustion of engines that have outlasted a revolution, outlasted Fidel, pushing into the future while dragging behind them the pungent odor of the past.

One day we drive through the neighborhoods west of the city center. Between Soviet-era apartment buildings, we see empty lots planted in vegetables. "State gardens," Yoli says. "From the Special Period." In the 1990s, after the collapse of the Soviet Union, the country became desperate. Cats, dogs and tree rats appeared on Cuban plates. A dinner of rice and a lollipop was common.

We pass the grand homes in Miramar where diplomats live and visiting foreign dignitaries stay. The streets are wide with manicured medians. Banyan tree tendrils reach for the ground. In the La Coronela neighborhood, the apartment buildings are utilitarian blocks—pink, blue, pale yellow. "Ninety percent military housing," Yoli says. Soon, we pass an impenetrable thicket of foliage, walls of it. It is rumored, Yoli says, to be the Castro residence.

The highway widens. Post-Revolution Havana recedes and I am once again in the Hera's longed-for Old World. We pass an orange and white 1954 Oldsmobile convertible with a pitted grill and paint that glosses in the sun. Its paint is thicker and a brighter color than it would have been then, new from the factory. On the shoulder, a herd of white goats grazes on dense mats of grass. A horse-drawn cart plods by. Nearby, a man in a bright orange tank top scythes a machete through tall grass. Wild sugarcane bows in a breeze. Cuba dissolves into the countryside.

Military plane displayed outside Havana's Museum of the Revolution

The Color of Words
Cyndi Goddard

"Those bearded bastards are pointing the goddam things straight at us."

I pressed my ear to my parents' closed bedroom door, trying to understand my father's words. He wanted my mother to pack up our station wagon and take us far away from Florida, to my grandmother's house in Ohio. At six years old, I was as frightened by father's anger as I was titillated by the lure of adventure in the back of the Rambler.

For two weeks in October of 1962, reruns of *I Love Lucy* were interrupted, Ricky Ricardo cut off mid-Babalú, by men in black suits, their white shirt cuffs brilliant against the vast gray space of the ocean projected behind them. I sat cross-legged on the floor in front of the TV, following the progress of ships full of missiles. My father said they were going to Cuba.

Cuba, our neighbor. We could take our boat to Cuba, if we trailered it and put in at the ramp in Key West. People did it all the time. My uncle often went fishing in Cuba. One of my parents' friends had just returned from a wedding there.

Cuba was right next to us on the globe, a small, green island in an ocean of blue. It would be so easy to miss it, I thought. If the ships went a little off course, they could crash into Florida with their deadly cargo. Who was doing this ... and why?

My father blamed the bearded, dark-haired men in army fatigues, fat cigars between their lips, whose faces leered from the newspapers lining my parakeet's cage. I didn't understand then that his fury was rooted in fear. He could not protect his family from the missiles in this island neighbor's backyard.

For me, the missile crisis was the first crack in the smooth confidence of childhood, pricking that bubble of egotistical innocence in which I floated, supremely ignorant of the complexity of the world. For the first time, I understood that the world beyond our home could enter our lives, and there was nothing my parents could do to protect me. Even after the ships turned back, and the superpowers formed secret accords without Castro, I hid a transistor radio under the covers, listening to staccato speeches that I was certain urged comrades to revolution.

Fifty-five years later, I peer out the window at off-white strips of land framed by foaming green and turquoise splinted waves. I long ago moved away from this peninsula of white sand beaches and royal palm trees. I have studied in Spain, sailed the coast of Mexico, bungie jumped in Costa Rica, and learned the downward dog in Puerto Rico, circling ever and ever closer to Cuba.

The airplane engines change pitch as we begin our final descent, slipping from one nation's airspace to another with no discernable difference in the view. The sense of familiarity begins in the sky.

When I deplane in Havana, I cannot find the words to communicate with the driver who has met me at the airport, holding a handwritten sign with the single word: Goddard, my name. I interpret the sign to mean, *Welcome. You're here at last, a guest, a visitor, an invader, a stranger to this land.*

Not a stranger. I know this place by the sky. It is a pale, pale blue, bleached by the sun. I rode my bike beneath this sky, a heat-white blue under which palm trees, jasmine, mango, hibiscus, papaya and taro grow—a blistered blue. It is Florida's sky, almost white, as if the sea has sucked out the color, as if the heat has stolen the incentive to blueness—depthless, a blank canvas.

"Blank, *blanco*, white," I try to explain the sky to the driver.

"*Claro*," he answers, which translates as "white," "clear," "bright," or "of course." Is he supplying the word my rusty Spanish is reaching for? Or is he saying, *Yes, of course, it is the sky*? The driver doesn't understand about the sky because to know this sky you must leave it. Only when you've lived under another sky for many years can you perceive this one.

In Havana, our small contingent of writers has a guide for the week. Yoli interprets not just the language, but her culture for us. I like having an on-demand source of knowledge. I am trying to understand everything from the economics of Cuba to the prevalence of the color red here.

Yoli interprets when Alfredo, a middle-aged Cuban whose features and manner reveal a deep weariness, unravels history from his side of the Florida Straits. He leans forward intently, his elbows on the red and white checked cloth covering the table of the *casa particular*— part boarding house, part B&B—where we are staying, and talks about the Special Period, after the fall of the Soviet Union and the withdrawal of Russian trade, when the Cuban populace rode bikes for lack of oil and grew thin for lack of food. Through Yoli, the historian speaks of the economic collapse, the scarcities and austerity measures. Shortages begat shortages, as manufacturing dried up, industrialized agriculture ground to a halt, and the daily struggle for basic necessities exhausted the people. They became vegans as meat and dairy disappeared from the marketplace. Organic farming in Cuba is not a luxury of plenty. It is the result of decades of deprivation, unlike in the United States, where in the 1990's, veganism and the organic food movements grew in popularity as lifestyle choices. Meanwhile in the United States, Congress under President George W. Bush enacted laws to further restrict trade with Cuba and prohibit private humanitarian aid to the country, in part, as a response to political pressure by Cuban-American immigrants.

I grew up with people who had fled Castro's Cuba. People like my high school Spanish teacher, Señor Hildago, a superintendent of schools in Havana, who had left everything behind. Or like my friend Roberto's grandfather, who had managed to escape with their family jewelry secreted in a place that, as far as I knew, should have been a one-way tunnel. The immigrants wanted their homes back, their position, their possessions. My friend Amy's uncle had lost a fortune when his nightclubs were seized.

The nightclubs and luxury hotels belong to the people now, as does Hemingway's Finca Vigia in San Francisco de Paula, thirty minutes outside Havana. The house is wrapped in reverence, like the suitcases at the airport, moribund in plastic, spun round and round, airtight, protected.

My group peers through Hemingway's windows at collections of animal heads, dishes, furnishings, room after room, the government guide narrating, Yoli interpreting, a double barrier thicker than the glass we press our faces against. According to the on-site guide's tremulous recitation, Ernesto's widow, Mary, gifted the house and its contents to the Cuban people.

Mary Hemingway gave a quite different accounting of seizure of her home, just as the guides in Hemingway's house in Key West offer visitors there an alternative view of the writer's life.

In Cuba, I begin to wonder if it is the translation that gives rise to contradictions or if reality is altered by the stories we tell and the words we use. Was the Cuban Missile Crisis shaped by the narrative our televisions showed us? And what of the Cuban people who hadn't known about it until four decades later when their leaders declassified the information?

When Alfredo, the historian, told us that most Cubans had been unaware of their nation's role in the standoff that brought our world to the brink of nuclear war, I stopped listening for a few minutes as I grappled with the fact that the people of Cuba had lived an alternate reality for forty years. We, U.S. citizens, who call ourselves Americans as if there were only one America, live in a world far, far different from the one ninety miles from our southernmost point.

Alfredo's revelations affect us all as he unveils incident after incident that we know nothing about. Unlike the Cubans, who are kept ignorant of the private lives of their leaders or their maneuverings on the world stage, we have access to this information, if we care to look. Books have been written about Operation Peter Pan—the exodus of over fourteen thousand unaccompanied minors from Cuba to the U.S., created by the Catholic Welfare Bureau in Miami—movies made about the Mafia's pre-Revolutionary grip on the country, stories abound on the effects of our fifty-five-year blockade, yet few North American realities include this knowledge.

My last night in Havana, I sit in La Taberna, a club in Habana Vieja, as performers swirl and spin, shake and shimmy in Latin rhythms we all think we know. The spectacle is colored by Yoli's cynicism. She has told us that the music that emanates from the bars and restaurants all over Havana is not an expression of Cuba's culture. It's all about money, she says. Fidel pulled the people out of the depths of the

Special Period by adding English, music and art to the country's curriculum to appeal to the world's tourists.

The hands of a master guitarist, ancient and weathered, move with blurring speed, the music an incantation, aching and calling, falling, faster, merging with the fluttering breath of the flautist and the ninety-year-old vocalist holding us rapt as his voice soars, powerful, enthralling. We, the audience, tourists, are caught in the net of his solo, not breathing until the singer releases us with his final, eternal note. I cannot believe this is just for the money.

Early the next morning, I am traveling in the front seat of a broken-springed taxi on the way to Matanza, ninety miles from Havana. Yoli, my personal guide now that the weeklong conference has ended, naps in the backseat.

The highway passes along an empty coast, dotted now and then with oil wells, the birdlike pumps pecking at the pristine surroundings. I ask the driver about the wells, surprising us all with my almost-coherent Spanish. It is coming back to me, words emerging from my subconscious, occasionally flowing; more often, stuck on my tongue.

In Matanza, we pick up a local guide, who speaks to me in careful Spanish, with only the occasional translation by Yoli. At each attraction, the onsite guide joins us. I am surrounded by Cubans and rapid-fire Spanish, which I parse into fragmented meaning, pieces of sentences, the ending lost in the next thought.

We ascend to the top of Montserrat for the view of Matanza between its two rivers and the sea before descending into the Caves of Bellamar, where we walk among crystalline pillars formed by the meeting of stalagmites and stalactites, cavern after cavern of sculptural shapes: fantastical faces, a Buddha, a pair of lions, dancing water frozen in mid-flow, fossils. I touch colors, smooth contours sparkling in the electric lights lining the tunnels while the three guides walk ahead, trailing verbs, tossing nouns and adjectives to each other.

If the recovery from the Special Period means the flourishing of art and music, literature and culture, then I, too, am part of the recovery, following my guides through the literary past and present in Matanza, where Cuban theater was born and Ediciones Vigeles publishes books glued together by hand, collages of words and art, repurposed pieces, the collaboration of artists and writers. Here words, like the musical notes, have solid, dancing incarnations, physicality and life and power. Words like *communism* and *revolution* are reconfigured into poetry on these pages.

Those same words shot back and forth between my parents in 1962 when my mother, eight months pregnant with her fifth child, refused to leave our home no matter what Fidel Castro did. *Revolution, reds, missiles, nuclear war* circled our dining table and plummeted to the cold terrazzo floor, shattering, the broken mirror of a neighbor no one understood, its sharp-edged shards reflecting the pale, pale sky.

I imagine the child I was slipping from her seat to clean up the jagged shards of understanding before her sisters' bare feet are slashed. I see the blood bead red on my fingertips as I attempt to assemble a mosaic from the splinters of socialism, communism, blockades, art, and music. It took fifty-five years and the traversing of that ninety-mile stretch of open water to do so.

A bartender at the Hotel Nacional

My Havana Hallucination
Robert Markowitz

I am at the Café Carlyle in Manhattan when I first hear the siren's call to Cuba. It is the early sixties and Bobby Short is at the piano playing "Sand in My Shoes."

> *Sand in my shoes, sand from Havana*
> *Calling me to that ever so heavenly shore*
> *Calling me back to you once more.*

Naïve and uninformed as I am—a boy disguised to myself as a young man—my head is filled with newsreel accounts of the People's Revolution and Fidel Castro's triumphant return to Havana. Hemingway has proclaimed himself a true Cuban and publicly kissed the national flag. I return home that night dizzy with anticipation of seeing it for myself.

Decades later, my plane slides onto the runway and the city outside my window with its flickering lights beckons. Bobby Short is dead. Hemingway has killed himself. And the romantic ambitions of my youth have come under the adult supervision of the President of the United States, the Secretary of State, and the Secretary of the Treasury.

The engine's roar does nothing to silence a dire and disquieting Greek chorus warning me to stay away. In an ironic twist on Homer's *Odyssey*, a tale in which sailors lash themselves to masts and plug their ears to avoid the enticement of a siren's song, U.S. diplomats in Havana are losing their hearing. The State Department blames Cuba, charging that someone—they're not saying who—has been launching sonic attacks on the embassy. The Secretary of State ordered U.S. diplomats home.

A thick packet of papers with restrictions from my government weighs heavy in my backpack. The U.S. Secretary of Treasury (with face and name so reminiscent of characters in *The Wizard of Oz* that I think of him as Secretary Munchkin) has forbidden Americans to patronize establishments controlled by the military. That includes most hotels, many restaurants, local stores—and the beaches. That is a worry. More worrisome is the feeling that I'm being watched. As I'm here with other writers, I'm required to have two minders—one American and the other Cuban—both of them making sure I don't stray from the itinerary.

I grab a taxi and we pass the embassy, which has all the appeal of a waffle iron. Fearful of a sonic attack, I tap-tap on my hearing aids. Still working. There is only the thunderous roll of the tropic sea floating in through the window. My fears recede into temporary remission.

I'm staying at a *casa particular*—in a room in someone's home. Parked outside the window my first morning, a line of vintage cars as glamorous as movie stars from the '50s stirs a memory from my childhood. Reincarnated as taxis in all the candied colors of melt-in-your-mouth M&Ms, they stand ready to begin the day: convertibles with their tops down, their chrome fins and hood ornaments glistening like silver-wrapped Hershey kisses, It is like being offered chocolates for breakfast: Fords and Chevys and Buicks and Pontiacs, maintained inside and out by ingenious Cuban mechanics who can fire up a combustion engine as easily as they can a woman.

Along with my minders I'm bundled into a carful of tourists. We race along the Malecón in a Chevy the color of turquoise, "Guantanamera" blasting from the dashboard, the smell of the ocean below, the sound of the waves splashing against the seawall, the sun in my eyes, the linger of rum on my lips. The touch of a lover's kiss.

> *You are the moonlit memory I can't seem to lose*
> *That's why my life's an endless cruise*
> *All that is real is the feel of the sand in my shoes.*

Until we turn the corner, and with the ride at an end I tumble into the arms of the crumbling city. The sidewalks are a hodge-podge of dislocated cobblestones treacherous even in daylight. Yoli, my Havana minder and official guide is, at age thirty-two, a combustion of boundless energy and crackling intelligence. To my question of what she thinks Cubans are most proud of, she does not hesitate. "Survival," she says.

I'm beginning to understand. Cuba is an island of survivors. An island of people who have little or nothing but who live as if they have everything. They are wise to the ways of the foreign nationals who come and go as regularly as the tides. The Americans who came for their sugar and rum and women and got tossed out by Castro and his Revolution; the Soviets who came for their hearts and minds and left them in poverty; the CIA that came for Castro again and again but failed. What survived—and still flourishes in Cuba today—are the seeds of suspicion and mistrust.

As a former filmmaker, I'm interested in what limitations, if any, are placed on Cuban filmmakers. Javier Recio, himself a survivor, is a young filmmaker and gifted artist whose arresting and colorful T-shirts are known throughout Cuba. Sitting with Javier outside a café on a Havana street corner, I tell him about a movie called *Soy Cuba (I Am Cuba)*, a film that is world famous but unknown to Cubans. Begun as a collaboration by Soviet and Cuban filmmakers in 1962, it tells the story of the Cuban Revolution in phantasmagorical images. It was shot in black and white with a wide-angle lens decades before the magic of current technology. It took two years to complete. *Soy Cuba* is a stunning achievement. One shot—which begins on a hotel rooftop and ends at the bottom of a pool—defies gravity.

"It is like witnessing a moon shot before the invention of the booster rocket. No one knows how it was done," I say.

"I never heard of it," Javier says.

Soy Cuba was screened simultaneously in Moscow and Santiago de Cuba. The film's Slavic sentimentality embarrassed the Cubans. The Soviets worried that scenes depicting the Cuban uprising were dangerous. It was never shown again, until 1993 when American filmmakers rediscovered it. Today *Soy Cuba* is regarded as a cinematic masterpiece. I hand him a copy.

"It will make you cry," I say.

"Being in Cuba you don't need a reason to cry."

The street is sunlit and the café latte sweet, but his words cast a shadow over the afternoon. I can only guess that Javier considers *Soy Cuba* part of a distant past and of little interest to a struggling young artist. The Revolution belongs to his parents' generation, not his.

"So tell me your story," I say.

"Which part?"

"The part about your film."

He tells me first about the Costa Ricans.

"There were two of them, both men," he begins. "They approached me and P. at our film festival in Camagüey."

P.—a director and producer—ran an artists' group there called La Resistancia. It was 2015, and they were preparing to make a movie. The Costa Rican visitors showed up unannounced, started hanging out with the group, asking questions about their artistic interests.

"We told them we were about shaping culture, not politics."

Javier tells me they said they were interested in supporting audio and visual projects. Before leaving, they asked P. what he needed.

"He said we need money and equipment," Javier says. "Then they left and we forgot about them."

A month later one of the men returned with what P. needed to make the film.

"What did they give him?" I ask.

"Eight hundred dollars, a GoPro camera, a new computer and an external hard drive."

Javier is watching me. "It was a lot," he says. It's as though he's afraid no American could appreciate what a Cuban filmmaker might achieve with eight hundred dollars and some camera equipment.

"You must have been thrilled," I say.

"I wasn't there. They called and asked P. to meet them in the park."

I am picturing the scene as I would a movie. A Cuban fairytale shrouded in intrigue.

The filmmakers thought they had what they needed. Then P.'s aunt called. She was watching the television news and a story had caught her attention.

"The Cuban police arrested two guys from Costa Rica and charged them with working for the CIA," Javier says. "There's a knock at P.'s door. It's the Security Police."

This is the movie they should have shot is what I'm thinking. But in Havana such thoughts are hallucinatory. "So what happened?"

"They questioned P. for two hours and let him go."

"That was it?"

"They kept the equipment and the money." Javier watches me. I wait. I know from his eyes there is more. He is a good storyteller.

"It took almost two months but we got back the equipment."

"But not the eight hundred dollars."

"They deposited it in an account to use in the production."

"Did you make your film?"

"We did."

"But you were being watched."

He smiles.

"The bartender is being watched," Yoli says. We are at the door to the bar in the government's Hotel Nacional.

Who's watching this time, I wonder, as we try to gain entry to the state-run establishment: the CIA or the Security Police? The bartender, like the one in Godfather II, is wearing a tux and holding an empty wine glass.

"There's a two-drink minimum here," Yoli says.

"So it's about money?"

"Yes."

We've come in from the outside patio where we sat to avoid buying drinks in the government bar. We have had two drinks. But they don't count, the barman says. He's not budging. Neither am I.

"There's a camera keeping track of his customers," Yoli says.

"Let's forget it." I've had enough watchers for one day. My thoughts are crowded with images of Javier and P. and the Security Police. I'm feeling Cuban.

Yoli completes her negotiation with the barman in Spanish. He hands her the empty wine glass.

"Okay," she says to me, "you'll have to buy two bottles of water."

Two bottles of water? Would that trigger an audit on my tax return? Secretary Munchkin is never out of mind. If I don't touch the bottles and don't drink the water, all they'll have is my fingerprints on an empty glass.

I reach into my wallet and pull out five CUCs, around five dollars, for the waters.

"Six," says the bartender.

I hand over the six CUCs. After all, the gang inside is worth the price of admission.

I came here to see the photographs.

Yoli accepts the bottles and hands me the empty wine glass. "In Cuba everything is possible. And nothing is possible," she says.

We enter the bar. Nowhere is the American past more present in Havana than on the walls of this bar.

"What do you see?" Yoli asks.

"I see dead people."

Dead movie stars: Brando before he was the size of a float in a Macy's Parade. Chaplin and Keaton, Mantle and DiMaggio, Sinatra and Ava, they all played and slept here. Nat King Cole sang here but was not allowed to sleep here. Nat King Cole was black.

"Who is that?" Yoli is looking at the little man in a fedora.

"That's Meyer Lansky, a famous Jew." I know because when I was a child my parents noted the name of every American Jew who had climbed out of anonymity into the limelight. When Meyer moved his gambling operations from Vegas to Havana, the Nacional was the crown jewel, and he ran it. Judging by his expression in the picture, he's still in charge.

I raise my empty glass. Back in the grand lobby Yoli hands me one of the bottles. Without thinking, I hand her my iPhone, open the bottle, and take a swig. Yoli snaps my picture. I'm smiling.

Outside the hotel I call for a taxi for the two of us.

"You'll have to tell him we're from New Zealand," Yoli says. "Otherwise they require four passengers." I do not ask why. This is Havana. Nothing is at it appears here. Is it an illusion I'm seeing or am I having a week-long hallucination?

On the way to the airport I review what happened. All that panic about sonic attacks at the U.S. Embassy turns out to be bogus. Oh, there was a problem—hearing loss, memory and mood problems—but no sonic waves. Just another unsolved mystery, more fodder for spying eyes which go back to Hemingway. Declaring his support of Castro and kissing their national flag went right into his FBI file. I am in good company.

I glance at the photo of myself drinking from the forbidden bottle of water and wonder, *Will this be the thing that nails me?* As we pass the Malecón and the beaches below I have only one regret. That I did not get sand in my shoes. But what if I had? And if the Customs guy ordered me to take off my shoes, what then? Going to the beach is on the restricted list.

When I arrive the gatekeepers at Immigration welcome me back. Customs waves me through. No one asks for my paperwork. I can keep my shoes on. My return is as seamless as a reentry from Toronto.

I am home and the season of paranoia has passed. I post the photo of me with the water bottle on my Facebook page. Now even the Russians have it.

If this had been a movie, who would have believed it?

Not me.

Sunflower-woman mosaic at Fusterlandia

Cuba through the Looking Glass
Laurie McAndish King

A long blue pool stretches across the center of the compound. It is surrounded by tall palm trees and slippery, red-lipped fish. Looking down from his home above the water, a laughing monkey sits atop the pregnant giraffe's back. Roosters spread their wings in the sun. Nearby, a gigantic strawberry-and-pistachio sundae with a cherry on top melts in the bright December light. There is no sound.

 I move silently, glad I wore my sneakers. It's still early, and I don't want to disturb the residents or draw attention to myself as I climb to the third story of the compound for a better look.

 Cowboys are everywhere. One wears heavy black mascara and blood-red lipstick. There is a fish where his heart should be. Another cowboy rides off on a dragon, his long blue cape blowing in the breeze. The mermaid in his arms does not look happy to be there; I think perhaps he is kidnapping her. A third cowboy stands, motionless, holding his bright red crutches. I skirt them all, one after another, making my way quickly to the top of the building where a huge red woman awaits, a golden sunflower sprouting from her head. Her tiny breasts poke out impertinently. The left one is bigger than the right. I lie down at the woman's feet and marvel at the deep blue beyond, a sky so clear and intense it reaches down and wraps itself around the woman.

This is Fusterlandia, a zany wonderland created by José Rodriguez Fuster over the course of more than forty years ... and he's still building it. Fuster's work has been compared with Gaudí's, Picasso's and Dubuffet's, and it's easy to see their influences in his fanciful mosaics, double-faced women and colorful naïve renderings. The renowned Cuban artist began by covering his own studio—a small wooden house in the seaside town of Jaimanitas—with colorful paintings and mosaics. When Fuster ran out of walls, he filled the yard with psychedelic sculptures: mermaids, palm trees, roosters and gigantic disembodied hands. Then he moved on, with permission, to cover more than eighty of his neighbors' houses with wildly ornate sculpture, painting and mosaic art. He was unstoppable, eventually decorating roofs, walls, gates, doorways, bus stops, benches and fountains.

Of course it wasn't just fun and games. When José Fuster first began expanding Fusterlandia in the town of Jaimanitas, the locals weren't all immediately appreciative. But that soon changed: It seems Fuster's effervescent spirit—his joy in creation—was irresistible. His art transformed an economically depressed village, well off the beaten track, into a fantasyland that attracts busloads of curious travelers. It's free to enter Fusterlandia, and it's easy to spend a little money on a souvenir tile or a painting in one of the many gift shops nearby. The whole town has benefitted—and bootstrapped itself to greater prosperity—as a result of Fuster's vision.

Near the red woman with a sunflower sprouting from her head I find the vantage point I am searching for. It's the epicenter of Fuster's kaleidoscopic dreamscape, and gives me a clear view of his Madonna. Rays of golden light emanate from her head as she clutches the child and a cross. To the Madonna's left, a green octopus waves its tentacles wildly. The three men carrying her in a rowboat do not seem concerned. Overhead, gigantic headless snakes curl, like sinuous rollercoasters, in dizzying loop-de-loops. A golden-eyed crocodile balances a bottle of beer on its back.

I spot a bench that is covered with white ceramic tiles and decorated with red hearts and blue flowers. Across the back is painted, in a childlike scrawl, *La alegria de vivir*. The joy of living. This is the first message of Fusterlandia.

Fuster credits the time he spent teaching literacy skills in the Sierra Maestra, a mountainous region of southeastern Cuba, for inspiring his art. The peasants, palm trees and crocodiles of that area still show up now—decades later—in his work. After that teaching experience in his late teens, Fuster trained for two years at the National School for Art Instructors in Havana. He's been working as a professional artist ever since. I am surprised to learn that "artist" is a state-approved profession, and it turns out that Cuba treats its artists well. Fidel Castro recognized early on that selling art—which is exempted from the trade embargo—was one of the few legal ways to get U.S. money into the country.

Cuban artists enjoy the same free education as students in other fields, and the subject is taken seriously. Printmaking, for example, has been an independent specialty in the education system since 1959. And in 1962, a printmaking collective was founded in Old Havana.

That collective, the Taller Experimental de Gráfica, is still standing, and it is one of my favorite places to visit. Even though it's run by the state, the Taller isn't a big warehouse full of food-rationing booklets or political propaganda. It's an enormous bunker-like cement building with high windows and a rough interior, and it's filled with art—really *good* art.

Near the entrance, just to the left, are the dancing coffeepots. In portrait after portrait they pose, often in pairs, bowing, primping and swishing; puffing themselves up to look more important; arguing, kibitzing or demurring. They get along fine without legs, and their heads often become daffodils.

I walk up the aisle, passing long tables loaded with paint samples—red, yellow, blue, green, orange—buckets, rollers, stacks of prints. I know where I'm headed: to a display of brightly colored, hand-painted-and-burnished prints. They're clipped up to horizontal strings in an improvised booth, to surround the viewer. The images are wild and beautiful, frightening in their intensity—a green cat, red and yellow stripes, fish with stars for eyes, darling hooves, blue reptilian skin—all layered into an exploding mythology unlike anything I have ever seen. Loaded with symbolism and gold foil, these pieces magnetize me from across the room and make my heart beat faster.

On one visit I meet a printmaker named Alejandro. He has worked at the Taller for twenty-six years and has a headful of wild hair, a charming gap between his front teeth, and speaks English well. Alejandro shows me several serigraphs in the series he is working on—colorful depictions of men in big, round, deep-sea diving helmets.

In one print, four divers labor beneath the water, harvesting seaweed with machetes. They wear orange diving suits and yellow helmets. Although they inhabit the same seabed, each diver is distinct, separated from the others, unable to communicate except perhaps with a few arm signals. Bubbles drift upwards, bright white circles against the dark kelp forest. Above the men—on the surface of the sea—a man relaxes in a rowboat, unaware of the alternate reality below. The style is completely different from that in Fusterlandia, but there's a haunting similarity in their imageries: innocent subjects in bright Caribbean colors distracting—at first—from a subtler message that things are more complicated than they first appear.

In another of Alejandro's serigraphs, a farmer ploughs his field in the slanting afternoon sun. It looks quietly idyllic until I realize the beast of burden is not an ox, but a rhinoceros. In a third print, a diver is wrapped in the red-white-and-blue Cuban flag, with a big red shield and the white Cuban star emblazoned over his heart. With up to eleven colors each, the prints are bright, lively and technically excellent.

Alejandro holds up the print of the four deep-sea divers to give me a better look.

"What's going on in this one?" I ask.

"These images show the difficulty of what we do every day," Alejandro says. "It's like we are living underwater, with limited oxygen, and every movement requires extra energy."

"That's what it feels like, living in Cuba?"

"That's what it feels like every day."

Once Alejandro has told me what the images mean to him, I realize those feelings have crept into me, too, as I view the divers: the claustrophobia of living underwater, the heaviness, the isolation. The fear just a breath away. I try to imagine what it would be like to have those feelings every day.

Since we're getting personal, I decide it might be OK to ask Alejandro a little more about how the financial system works in Cuba. "Do you earn a salary for your work here?" I venture.

"Yes, of course!" he replies, looking a little bewildered.

I feel both foolish and incredulous—it's hard to believe the government would pay printmakers to create art—not government publications, but *art. Any art. Whatever they want.* No one seems to be looking over Alejandro's shoulder, telling him not to show what it looks like to live underwater, not to comment on the extra energy required for everyday activities. It's true that there was censorship in the early '70s, but since then things have opened up. Since the '90s, Cuban art has included more explicitly political content and even critiques of the Revolution.

"And do you also get paid when the prints are sold?" I ask, still finding it hard to comprehend the extent of this government-funded enterprise.

"Yes, we get to keep seventy percent of the sale price; the government gets the other thirty percent to pay for the space—it's expensive to keep the lights on and do regular maintenance."

The Taller Experimental de Gráfica is not the only art hot-spot in Havana. The Museum of Cuban Art displays world-class painting; the Fabrica de Arte Cubano combines art, fashion and music; and many of the streets in Old Havana—especially Empedrado—are home to quirky little galleries and individual artists' studios: A super-realist paints faux broken panes of glass over his seascapes. A portrait artist evokes intense anguish with black-and-white faces. A photographer specializes in the upside-down worlds reflected in water.

Even the graffiti and street art in Cuba are full of symbolism and mystery. Yulier Rodríguez, who signs his work Yulier P, has populated the streets of Old Havana with space-alien-like creatures: bald, big-headed beings whose body parts aren't assembled properly. Many include visual references to hunger: creatures with many breasts, or mouthless ones. Some critics speculate that the mouthlessness implies a lack of voice and refers to artistic censorship. That's certainly possible; the police keep track of Rodriguez's work, and subjected him to an interview about it. They didn't arrest him, though. The Cuban constitution guarantees his right to create art—as long as it doesn't oppose the Revolution.

Another artist, who works semi-anonymously, paints a balaclava-clad character accompanied by the phrase "2 + 2 = 5." I ask Yoli, our local guide, what that means—maybe *Something isn't adding up*? She asks friends, but no one seems to know.

Later I read an article that said the signature phrase was a direct reference to a line in Orwell's *1984*: "In the end the Party would announce that two and two made five, and you would have to believe it…. Not merely the validity of experience, but the very existence of external reality, was tacitly denied by their philosophy." Of course, that could refer as easily to the current U.S. administration's claims about "fake news" and "alternative facts" as to Cuban censorship.

But the artist himself is circumspect, perhaps because that is still the safest stance. In one interview he is quoted as saying the phrase is simply a childhood nickname; in another he says it represents freedom: "People say that two plus two equals four, but I don't see it like that. I believe that it can equal whatever you want it to be. You can be whatever you want to be… And I want people to know that, so I put it everywhere with my art. I paint here, I paint there, I paint everywhere. I want people to know that I am free."

I've been thinking a lot about Cuban art since my conversation with Alejandro. Its generally naïve style, frequently fantastical subject matter and usually inoffensive approach might seem to say, *Don't take me seriously*. But underneath, for those who know how to read them, other messages await. Cuban artists express themselves in code; their work speaks on multiple levels. A second monkey perches on the elephant's head.

The woman's body becomes a cross.

2 + 2 = 5.

A Santería fortuneteller and her client talk in Havana's Parque de la Fraternidad

True Blood
Adrienne Amundsen

To dive into the beating heart of Cuba, you must see the dying heart of the chicken sacrificed in a Santería ceremony—at least that is what I discovered.

People have strong reactions when I mention Santería. They associate it with Voodoo, animal sacrifice, even devil worship. I wanted to understand its darker aspects, but also the spiritual path it embodied. I wanted to find out what was true, what lay beneath the surface. How could I go to Cuba and ignore Santería?

Finally in Cuba, I missed its first appearance: a chicken head my travel companion Laurie saw on the sidewalk as we enjoyed an introductory walk through Old Havana. The next sighting, however, was impossible to ignore. The Parque de la Fraternidad—Brotherhood Park—was planted with soil from every country in the continent. In its center was a magnificent ceiba tree, one that our guide Yoli told us was sacred to Santería. Its trunk reached tall into the clear sky, leaves flickering in the sun. Its roots spread and twined in graceful waves. But there, nestled amongst the beautiful roots, were chicken feathers, bones and white plastic bags stained with blood—sacred offerings to the Orisha, the gods of Santería. On benches around this tree sat several large women in white, crowned with colorful turbans—Santería fortunetellers. Cloth dolls perched on the backs of their benches, and on the ground before each woman lay a blanket set with candles and cards. I was, of course, eager for a reading. But I was shy, and our group was moving on.

"How would you understand it anyway if you don't speak Spanish?" asked MJ, a fellow traveler.

"I don't know—I just want the experience." I wanted a whiff, a taste, a shiver. I imagined slipping into a not-unfamiliar trance, carried away by sound and energy.

The Yoruba religion, practiced in Western Africa, particularly in Nigeria, made its painful way to Cuba and South America on slavers' ships. Bringing their religion with them, the slaves had to practice it in secret. To be safer, they "syncretized," or combined Yoruba with Catholicism. Thus each Yoruban Orisha is identified with a Catholic saint: African gods hiding in plain sight! The Cuban form of Yoruba is called Santería. This is an old religion practiced in the "New World" by people torn by generations of trauma. Given years of enslavement and violence, it is hardly surprising that it has a dark and bloody undercurrent. Perhaps their experience contributed to what Tobe Melora Correal, in her book *Finding Soul on the Path of Orisa*, calls "the well of fear-driven appeasement" of vengeful ancestors practiced through anxious sacrifice and empty ritual, rather than a religion identified with openness, trust and love. I struggled with similar issues in the religion of my childhood, filled with so much fear of hellfire and damnation that the experience of a loving God was often lost. But instead of throwing away religion altogether, I have looked for teachings not rooted in fear. Similarly, Correal describes finding a Santería practice free of such fear, a religion of great beauty and magic. Would I, too, find this in Cuba?

Our guide's family, I learned, had practiced the religion for generations. Yoli confided that she'd left the religion because it held no appeal for her, was too full of fear and endless rituals. Nevertheless, she promised to take me on the next step in my journey. I was just coming out of our morning writing workshop when she rushed up and said, "If you want to go to a Santería celebration, we need to leave right now. Today is the feast day for Chango, and there will be music in Hempel Alley between 12 and 1. We gotta go!" We grabbed a couple of others and ran for a cab, while Yoli told me more about Chango: that he is the "macho god," the Lord of Fire and Lightning, of war, music and drumming; that his color is red.

We spilled out of the cab at the opening to an alley filled with art and music—psychedelic murals on faded multi-colored walls, totem-like metal art, masks, and tall trees raining dappled light and shadow on the crowded, drum-drenched scene. A fortuneteller in a gold satin turban and a rich ruby-red skirt leaned over a small table draped with white, reading someone's cards. Under a blue and green canopy, women in tight yellow T-shirts and skirts or cut-offs, and muscular men in yellow and red drummed fiercely on bright yellow *djembes*. Others kept the rhythm on hollow wooden instruments. People danced with extraordinary grace in front of the drummers, and everyone circling around the makeshift stage moved with the contagious rhythms. Here was Afro-Cuban dance and music in its authentic spiritual context. The music had a magnetic pull on me, but Yoli whisked us back down the alley through a dark door into a small courtyard room filled with strange sights: a metal construction of old rusted film reels, a bronze propeller, a gold-painted face on a hat stand, and a giant upright drill; an ancient tricycle; an exotically painted white-washed basin embedded in the brick wall. A trio of Conga drums sat waiting to be brought to life by their drummers. In the corner, where a tree grew up through the roof, rose an altar to the ancestors. Mounted low on the tree trunk a gold Madonna perched, holding the Christ child. Leaning against the facing wall stood a peeling picture of Che on a sea-green background. What better Cuban Chango than Che?

The proprietor, apparently an expert in Santería, was distracted by several people who seemed to have business with him, but promised to tell me more later in the day if I returned.

I made my first mistake later that day at the Parque Almendares, a lush green park bisected by a swiftly flowing river where emerald vines poured down the trunks of wide-limbed trees. The light was golden-green; it felt like a fairytale forest. But a faint sour smell marred the magical feeling, and when I looked down, I saw garbage strewn about. This time it wasn't just chickens in white plastic bags. There were dried animal skulls with long feathers attached, and splatters of blood. To my left lay an entire beheaded goat carcass, its brown and white fur still soft and shiny.

I began snapping pictures of everything I saw. When I spotted a small group of people in long white dresses nearing the river down below, I raced to get near enough to see. I knew I should show respect, hang back, but I couldn't help myself. I wondered about my need to "capture" something in a photo. The worshippers at the river were quietly singing and chanting, and submerging themselves under the water. Several carried cloth-covered baskets. Did these hold sacrificed animals or their body parts? Why were animals still sacrificed in these ceremonies when the practice had largely ended elsewhere? I thought of the goat's body lying on the ground up the hill and the blood around the ceiba tree.

I pulled back from my frantic photo shoot and walked on, hoping that the celebrants wouldn't see me. I could have erased the pictures, but I didn't. Returning to the stairs where we had entered the park, to my surprise and chagrin, Yoli had gathered the people in white and told them I'd like to talk with them. They were friendly and open. They told me that they made sacrifices to show God gratitude, and that it was a long, demanding process to be fully initiated into the Santería priesthood. For example, initiates may commit to regular prayers honoring their guiding Orisha, or give up sex for several years. Some here had been raised in Santería families; one joined as an adult, wanting to be on a path connecting him to *"el divino, lo sagrado"*— the divine, the sacred. And no need to be sneaky: They invited me to have my picture taken with them. We hugged each other good-bye.

While I had explored other ceremonial practices, lost myself in music and shamanic communion with ancestors and gods of different kinds, there was something more mysterious and foreign about Santería for me. I felt like an outsider. The blood sacrifices, the Orisha, the highly developed complex songs and ceremonies, the African roots, the backdrop of slavery—I felt at a respectful remove.

In Santería there is one single Supreme Being or Source named Olorun whose work in this galaxy is carried out by the Creator Olodumare. They exist in an invisible realm. The Orisha are their helpers, divine immortals on earth, here to help us. The energies of the Source flow through the Creator and from the Creator into the Orisha. This energy is called *ashé*.

Practitioners learn the teachings of Santería from experienced elders. This is an oral tradition, not a religion "of the book." Ceremonies involve intense ritualized chanting, drumming, singing and dancing. Santería is also a "possession" practice. In the throes of ecstatic music and dancing, people are open to being *taken over* by the spirit of an ancestor or orisha, or "ridden" by them. This experience is cleansing and illuminating, the deepest communion with emissaries from the spirit world.

Much later in the trip, I finally had my chance to sit with a fortuneteller. She sprayed rose water all over me, raised her hands to the sky and invoked *la luz*. Her presence was dignified and strong. In a guttural and resonant voice, she spoke words in Spanish and chanted in Yoruba. Then she handed me the cards and asked me to cut them. Laying them out, she told me I was very connected to the spirit world, and predicted good fortune and much learning, then placed the blue beads of Yemaya over my head. I caught the whiff, the shiver, the scent! I felt the power in these women. Yemaya was whispering to me.

But my final and most powerful destination was the modest Santería Museum. There, old stairs led up to a spacious room filled with a giant sculpted tree and life-sized statues of the Orisha. Excited, I rushed forward and snapped a picture. Only then did I see the "no photography" sign and the little woman sitting by the stairs. She rose and raced toward me in a fury, grabbed my phone, yelled at me, and indicated that I must erase everything on it. I didn't need to speak fluent Spanish to understand that she wanted to keep my phone and banish me from the museum. I apologized sincerely, then obsequiously, and finally showed a little anger as she veritably pummeled me with outrage. But I got it. I had now been told in no uncertain terms that I needed to show respect and give up on "capturing" my precious images.

After that, she relented, and accompanied me. When she allowed me to stop in front of the first diorama displaying the main father god, Obolito, I was swept away by his beauty, by the energy. I stooped to read every word on the information card describing him.

The woman continued to follow me closely, glowering. I turned and smiled at her and asked her if Obolito was the father god. She nodded curtly. I moved on to the next figures and turned to tell my suspicious guardian that they were beautiful and powerful. Slowly she seemed to relax. "Oh, you are really interested!" she said with some surprise.

"Yes," I replied. "Very much!" I patted my heart and then put my hands together in prayer position … and she smiled.

After this, rather than following me like a guard, she accompanied me like a guide. The last two figures I reached before closing time were Oshun and her mother Yemaya. Oshun is the river goddess. Yemaya is her mother and the mother of all living things, the queen of heaven, earth and all her waters, especially the ocean. Her color is blue, the color of the beads my psychic reader had placed around my neck. I showed the beads to the woman shadowing me, and pointed from them to Yemaya. She nodded and smiled again. I was falling in love with Yemaya and decided that I would learn as much as I could about her. She would be my teacher, my guide. The museum was closing. The woman whisked me out, but now she was smiling. And she gave me my phone back.

Our trip was coming to a close. I had to leave the land of Santería behind, but when I got home, I dove into studying Yemaya. I made an altar to her, using shells and salt water, fruit offerings, and several cards and gifts I had recently received with images of the ocean and of mermaids, also sacred to the goddess. I learned prayers to her, and listened to music and chanting dedicated to her, with those wondrous Afro-Cuban beats. I took a ritual bath with sea salts, with seven candles burning, and reflected on the qualities of the shining upper layers of the ocean and the feelings I had when I was near the sea. I asked for her help to calm my fears.

On New Year's Day, I went to the furthest end of Point Reyes with my family. It was a clear blue day, rare that far out on the coast, and we walked to a vista point with the ocean all around. Whale spouts were barely visible out in the swells and whitecaps, and the surface of the ocean was luminous blue and silver. I am a worrier. I worry about everything. But standing there, hearing the waves below and resting my eyes on the distant horizon, I thanked Yemaya for the spiritual bounty of the ocean, the feeling of calm and sense of vastness in which my worries dissolved.

Ashé.

I love your empty highways and clean streets ...

Falling for Havana
Christine Berardo

Let me count the ways:
I love walking your darkened streets at night,
the meager streetlamps,
shadows dancing on crumbling *edificios*.

I love your glassless windows that let pass
the warm air of morning,
the torpor of hot afternoons.

I love walking amid your throngs,
comfortable in their own skins
every color of the palette,
cream to ebony, unafraid
to bare this flesh, this human shell
housing the soul of struggle,
of suffering
of survival.

I love your sounds:
the calls of street vendors below our window,

the warning trill of bicycle pedicabs—Outta my way!
the lapping and crashing of the sea
against your curving Malecón,
throb of music from open doorways,
the syncopated rhythms of carts
on broken cobblestones.

I love your buildings, broken and pocked
like faces of old women once young and glamorous,
unyielding beneath fresh layers of paint—
blue, pink, yellow, green, magenta—
standing proud despite gaping wounds
of want and neglect.

I love your empty highways and clean streets,
the lush green valleys and farms beyond your flanks,
towering royal palms and ceiba trees,
rivers and huts and artists making art of scraps,
and the cars from my childhood still cruising
six decades after rolling off that assembly line in Detroit.

I love feeling safe under your prying eyes,
no gun, no knife, no drunk driver
waiting in the crowd or around the bend.

And your people, the children of your troubled past?
Ah, how do I presume to say?
I hardly know them yet
but what I see, I love:
their hope, their belief in a future

still unrealized,
their cunning dodges to state sanction
and shameless joy and brawls over baseball,
their resourcefulness when that's all they have,
their refusal to flee
or give in to despair
or succumb—not to empires nor tyrants
not to Mafiosi nor state security
not to *el bloqueo* nor *el embargo*
nor friends bearing missiles
nor Uncle Sam luring away their children
nor broken promises and false smiles

but instead, oh instead, to see us coming,
stretch out their arms and smiling say,
"Bienvenidos, amigos, bienvenidos."

The author with Hemingway at El Floridita

Hemingway, Cuba and Me

Anne Sigmon

Do not go gentle into that good night,
Old age should burn and rave at close of day;
Rage, rage against the dying of the light.

—Dylan Thomas, "Do Not Go Gentle Into That Good Night"

The two *Papa dobles* knocked me on my ass. Those sour grapefruit daiquiris had a surprising kick. Since they were *his* favorite, I should have known. The crowd was three deep at the bar, everyone grooving to an all-girl salsa band at El Floridita, the Havana nightspot world famous as Hemingway's preferred watering hole. Barkeeps in red waistcoats churned out daiquiris a dozen at a time, sliding them down the timeworn mahogany surface of the bar.

I had no business being there: me, a brain-damaged stroke survivor maxed out on blood thinners. Drinking of any kind was dicey—much less carousing in a bar. I knew I was pushing it, and I didn't care. I was drawn to Cuba to feed my decades-old fascination with Ernest Hemingway as both writer and fearless adventurer, and to explore why I still loved him when much of the critical world had turned to harsh reappraisal.

I fell in love with Hemingway in freshman American lit. After two semesters of gruesome encounters with a headless horseman and Henry James's mind-numbing parlor games, I pulled an all-nighter reading Hemingway's *A Farewell to Arms*—not because I'd fallen behind, but because I'd fallen in love.

In college and the years beyond, I admired the tension of Hemingway's spare prose; I was captured by its romance. But what I truly loved was the raw adventure: the hot breath of the leopard, the marlin exploding from the Gulf Stream, breaking to run free.

Now, when I look back, I realize that I'd been fascinated by the Hemingway mystique even before I knew his name. When I was fourteen—while my junior high girlfriends swooned over posters of the Fab Four—my room sported a thirty- by sixty-inch poster of a handsome matador swirling his blood-red cape at a charging bull. A flamenco dancer stood to the side. Sitting there on my bed, I could almost hear the swish of her red ruffled dress and the clap-clap-clapping of her castanets. I don't remember why I chose that poster. All I knew then was that it represented the kind of adventure I craved.

Years later, I found my romantic hero in my husband, Jack. He hunted, he fished, he hiked rugged trails. Before I met him, he'd run with the bulls in Pamplona. He even looked like Hemingway. I was smitten.

Adventure was Jack's style. In Michigan, we read the Nick Adams stories, then crashed our canoe on the churning whitewater of the Pigeon River. On a six-day climb of Mt. Kilimanjaro, we snuggled in our sleeping bags, reading *The Snows of Kilimanjaro* by flashlight. On safari in Kenya, we stalked big game with our cameras, reading *The Green Hills of Africa* in the afternoon heat. We hit Pamplona for the Feria, and Jack ran with the bulls again. Afterward, wearing our red neck scarves, we sat at Café Iruña reading *The Sun Also Rises*.

That had all been years ago. Our vacations are tamer now. We are older, of course, and I am more fragile. In addition to stroke deficits and blood thinners, I'm embroiled in a lifelong battle with a nasty autoimmune disease. I've made concessions, but nothing could force me to pass up Cuba. Last year, with the loosening of United States travel restrictions, I set off. Though disappointed that Jack couldn't join me, I was determined to have the "full Hemingway" experience.

As I nursed my second *Papa doble* at El Floridita's bar, I studied the life-sized statue standing at the far left corner—Hemingway's spot. Frozen in bronze, the rugged writer stood, elbow on bar, radiating a mischievous charisma. I swear there was even a twinkle in his eye. A bronze notebook sat on the bar next to a real daiquiri glass. Much as it charmed me, the scene seemed somehow wrong. As I finished my drink, it hit me: The bronze Hemingway at El Floridita sports that iconic close-cropped beard so much associated with his image. But—remembering his biography—I realized that, by the time he grew the beard, he'd lost the twinkle. By then, he was deep into his querulous "Papa" period. In public, he was often drunk or rude or both.

He wasn't like that when he first came to Cuba. "The man I remembered was kind, gentle, elemental in his vastness," his third and youngest son Gregory once wrote.

Hemingway visited Cuba regularly for eleven years, to hole up and write in peace at the Hotel Ambos Mundos, to party with friends at El Floridita and to fish the Gulf Stream for marlin. In 1940, he made Cuba his home when he bought a fifteen-acre farm—La Finca Vigía—in the village of San Francisco de Paula, about ten miles southeast of Havana. He made friends with the local fisherman, doted on his menagerie of dogs and six-toed cats, and recruited village boys to play baseball with his three sons: John, Patrick and Gregory.

The day after I visited El Floridita, I set off down the Carretera Central to see Hemingway's home for myself. The house is hidden in a serene woodland of royal palms, bamboo, fig trees and mangos. Bright-pink bougainvillea and scarlet fireweed bloom in the garden.

The one-story Spanish colonial house is the color of pale sunshine. Tall windows and French doors open to the breeze that Hemingway loved. Inside, the house is a temple to his vast intellect and interests. In room after room bookcases sag with the weight of thousands of his books. The walls are crowded with hunting trophies and paintings. The place felt eerily familiar—the travel keepsakes, the books, the art reminded me of my own home, a testament to Jack's decades of globetrotting and mine.

Hemingway had several desks at the Finca, but his preferred spot was a simple bedroom where he wrote standing up using the top of a bookcase for a desk. I paused there to breathe in the magic at the shrine of his rusting Royal typewriter.

Hemingway loved Cuba and some say he did his best writing there. In his early days on the island, he wrote much of *For Whom the Bell Tolls*, my personal favorite of all his novels. But after its publication in 1940, he faced a tortuous twelve-year creative drought aggravated by a series of injuries. His "juices" weren't flowing. At the Finca, he set out to write the most audacious work of his life: a sweeping trilogy of sea, land and air. He never finished it.

Many scholars cite Hemingway's notorious drinking, plus a family tendency to bipolar depression, for his late-career slump. Malicious whispers charge that he allowed his fame to eat him alive.

But a new book, *Hemingway's Brain* by forensic psychiatrist Dr. Andrew Farah, says otherwise. Although there is no question that

Hemingway was an alcoholic, Farah concludes that his primary illness was dementia brought on by repeated head injuries. Farah identifies the disease as CTE (chronic traumatic encephalopathy), the same brain affliction currently getting worldwide attention for its crippling effects on football players and other athletes. It's progressive, devastating and, even today, there is no treatment and no cure.

Ever the macho (but accident-prone) adventurer, Hemingway suffered at least nine serious concussion injuries in twenty-five years, Dr. Farah found. They ranged from the World War I explosion that almost killed him at age eighteen, to car wrecks, boat accidents and the two plane crashes in 1954, from which he never recovered. In addition to broken bones and internal injuries, he suffered double vision, memory loss, slowed thought. And headaches that "used to come in flashes like battery fire," Hemingway wrote in a letter. These were "classic and typical symptoms of head trauma," Farah said.

As Hemingway's brain deteriorated over the last years of his life, he found it harder and harder to write.

I imagined him standing there in his bedroom at the Finca. Wearing old moccasins and a ratty shirt, he stood on a tattered animal skin rug at this writing station. A clipboard and his Royal typewriter perched on a sagging white bookcase that faced the wall. The author didn't need the Royal to keep up with the staccato rhythm of words blazing through his mind. He was focused on the nub of a pencil jabbing in frustration at an empty page. Did he hear the birds singing in the garden, palm trees rustling in the breeze? Did he notice his favorite cat, Boise, purring on the bed? Or was he consumed by the silence in his head?

During my stay in Cuba, I re-read his book *Islands in the Stream*, one of only two he set in his adopted home. The book was published (against his wishes) after he died. It's the story of a lonely artist who—

much like Hemingway himself—is divorced with three sons who visit during the summer. He has many friends, but when the boys aren't around, this man's most cherished companion is his cat. As the action lulled, I paged ahead. Then suddenly, the writer found his purchase and launched into a riveting scene. Bursts of gripping prose sparked terror as a shark stalked the youngest son.

There were also heartbreaking flashes of self-awareness as writer and protagonist seem to merge. The Hemingway-esque character describes aggression welling up like a tide. "He could feel it all coming up …. He did not know what made him feel the way he did …. It was as if he were hooked to a moving anchor." He chides himself: "You faker. You cheap phony. You rotten writer and lousy painter." The more Hemingway struggled to write, the more surly he became.

Then, suddenly, the fog cleared. In one final, epic clash, Hemingway fought the ocean of his unruly prose until it gave up Santiago, his *Old Man and the Sea*. In this book there was no drinking, no conversation, no railing at fate—just one exhausted old man battling for his life with supreme determination. In a six-week creative explosion, Hemingway honed a story that had been percolating in his mind for decades into one of the finest performances in modern literature. The book, published in 1952, resurrected Hemingway's career and propelled him to the Nobel Prize in 1954.

His moment didn't last. Recently I watched a television interview taped just two years after he finished his masterwork. Hemingway's struggle with language is heartbreaking. In the video, he looks down, speaks slowly, almost woodenly, at one point dictating punctuation as though he's writing. I winced, seeing him fight to fish words up from the depths in a brain-damaged effort I recognized all too clearly.

Not long after I returned home from Cuba, melancholy fell over me like a blanket. I was tired, sick of Hemingway and sick of myself. I was sad to be reminded of the misery that shadowed the last ten years of the author's life. Plus, I had my own secret torment: I couldn't write this story. Over the past two years, my cognition—damaged by that stroke fifteen years ago—has been steadily slipping. Words are harder to find; my typing grows more atrocious every day. I am too easily overwhelmed. Papers pile up in my office. Whittling a story from a box full of notebooks is a monstrous task. I feel like I am slipping toward the edge of my mind. Despite many consultations with doctors, no one can tell me how to stop the slide. Instead of lashing out like Hemingway, I drift. I ignore the phone, cancel dates and burrow into myself.

Suddenly I understand what had happened to Hemingway with *Islands in the Stream* and his other unfinished books. He could no longer manage his material. He couldn't separate the tip of his story from the gargantuan iceberg below.

Hemingway once said that writing had given him the greatest pleasure he'd ever known. The loss of his memory and, finally, his ability to write, propelled him inevitably toward suicide.

"Sometimes madness can be more frightening than death," his son Gregory wrote. "Papa had never been afraid of much and I respected his decision."

After Cuba, I felt a different kind of kinship with the writer I'd adored in my youth. I don't share his colossal talent, his outsized personality or his vicious demons. Still, I know the terror of sensing my mind fading away.

In his last years, Hemingway roared like a wounded bear. I forgave him for that, and the forgiveness deepened my appreciation of his work. He'd known all along what was happening to him, just as I know what's happening to me.

In tormented dementia, Hemingway, the man, did not go gentle into the night. As for me, I hope I'll handle it differently. I'm praying for the qualities shared by his best characters: courage and grace under pressure.

The world is a fine place … I hate very much to leave it.
—Ernest Hemingway, *For Whom the Bell Tolls*

Fisherman as the sun rises

Moments in Havana

MJ Pramik

Dedicated to *Thanasis Maskaleris*

never now
the eyes of Havana
      dusk along the Malecón

land of poets
afternoon light welcomes
      my life yet again

calle Obispo
dimming lights grow huge
      pulsed by salsa, shaken by rhumba

el Malecón
fishermen as the sun rises
      lovers as darkness falls

Wandering in Cuba

at Viñales we danced salsa
dined on roasted chicken, dark rum
    savored the green mountains

gnarled wiring, black octopus
above my casa's door
    genius of Cuban survival

I see you, my Greek poet
touching paint peeling off doors
    gates to heaven

so it was you
who walked with me
    along the Malecón each morning

    I'd forgotten you said
    you would accompany me.

The author and her Permit

An Old Woman and the Sea

Sandra Bracken

The memory I carry with me is from long ago. I was in Belize. Nothing cements a sense of place, creates an enduring memory, a connection, as holding onto a twenty-pound fish two hundred feet from the end of a fly rod, for thirty minutes. She is in control. She creates the dance, the moves, the duration. If you ask me what it was about that day or why she is so special, I cannot say exactly. It was not just the fight or the fear that she would go over the edge of the reef and cut the line on a piece of coral. Was it the exhilaration that when finally holding her, she was patient and allowed me my moment—motionless, her liquid silver stillness in my hands—so unlike other fish eager to leap or squirm free? I was transfixed by her large, round, penetrating eye, only a few inches from mine. Did she sense that I had never held a fish like her and how grateful I was? Did she know I was going to return her to the water? Was it my imagination that I sensed an equal admiration for me?

She is my siren song. I fear she will be my undoing as I continue my search. I fear time is not on my side.

I hoped to find my Permit (*Trachinotus falcatus*), in the waters off the island of Cayo Largo, southwest of the island of Cuba. I'd heard that the waters surrounding Cuba hold many of the lovelies I seek, that Permit are abundant and unafraid. I waited years for the opportunity; waited for the restrictions on American fishermen to change. When finally the political circumstances eased, I made plans for the trip.

In anticipation, I pored over maps and charts of the area of Isla Cayo Largo and reviewed the selection of flies recommended for my Permit. The list included invented variations of shrimp and crab flies that resemble the delicacies they impersonate or mimic their movement. As I turned each one over in my hand, I could see myself standing in the bow of a flats boat; completing a perfect cast into the crystal-clear waters of the Caribbean. The fly of choice in Cuba is the Avalon Fly, a shrimp imitation that was invented by the director of Cuban Fly Fishing Operations. My favorite, though, is Cathy Beck's Crab, named after its inventor, light beige with spindly rubber legs. All my flies would be carefully tied by my husband—a good luck omen.

I was going to Cuba to fish. After a brief stop in Havana, there was a short flight on a small Russian plane to the island. I've noticed that often the first day of fishing is the most disappointing—I go with too many expectations. And this first day was no exception. Winds were blowing twenty-five to thirty-five knots, gusting to forty-five. Waves occasionally broke over the stern and gunwales of the shallow nineteen-foot boat. I spotted several groups of small fish moving speedily through the water, probably Jacks and Bonefish. However, I had come for Permit; there was surely a Permit out there waiting for me. But the weather was not promising and if it didn't improve, we would never meet.

The wind continued through the night. The rain came in heavy sheets. Palm trees swayed chaotically. In the morning I learned the port was closed; no boats were permitted to go out. The airport was closed, too. Throughout the day the rain continued and winds escalated. I heard that a tropical storm was coming from Honduras and would take days to pass through. I found it hard to be optimistic.

There really was no chance of having a good fishing day when I finally went out if the weather did not change and the wind did not ease up. This was "flats fishing." In shallow water, it's about the hunt, about visibility, about being able to see the fish. And once found, it's about getting the cast, the fly, in the right place. I thought about the Permit, so sensitive to changes in barometric pressure. A front such as what we were experiencing sends them into deep water. They don't want be on the flats looking for food. Ever optimistic and ignoring this basic knowledge, I continued to search the shallows for tails of feeding fish or shadows under the surface: a Permit often joins a group of feeding Bonefish or accompanies a Sting Ray on the chance it might unearth a crab.

Lifting my eyes from the water, I could see hints of purple in the darkening grey sky, a dramatic backdrop to the white herons and sea eagles in flight. Nearing some mangroves I chuckled to myself at how much they resembled triffids—the tall, fictitious, carnivorous plants that can "walk" like a man on crutches. A long line of Australian pines marked the shore of an island. I remembered the complaints of a man I met in the Bahamas. Those pines, he said, were thought to stabilize shorelines because they grow fast, but their shallow roots do not trap sand and they crowd out native dune plants, actually increasing erosion. I pondered all of this before lowering my eyes to the water again. Nervous water ahead … hopefully Permit? I cast without knowing. The wind played havoc with my line, grabbing it and tossing it six feet off target. Whatever had stirred the water was gone. My dreams that night were focused on empty waters.

The following morning there was no change in the weather, winds a steady forty knots. The cooing of a dove was somehow soothing and lifted my spirits. Perhaps in a few sheltered bays there would be fish searching for refuge. I, too, was hoping to be in the lee of land, away from the wind where I'd have a better opportunity to cast. A high coral shore caught my interest. I thought it would be nice to go ashore, to explore. It was an idle thought. I hoped it wasn't going to be a day for reminiscing only.

The turtle grass colored some of the bottom greenish brown. Other areas were turquoise or baby blue—the talcum sandy bottom reflecting the sky. Those changes never ceased to surprise me. Fish are scarcely visible on the turtle grass. Seeing nothing below I looked to the sky. I had never seen so many frigate birds: forty soaring effortlessly high above, hanging as if suspended from invisible threads in the sky. I remembered the first time I saw one in Mexico. In those early days of fishing, each outing was an exotic adventure. A frigate bird was part of a new world, and I was like a child exploring that new world, my new skills, pleased with my abilities. It didn't really matter whether I caught a fish or not. I wanted to be on the water under the wide-open sky. I had no expectations. That was then. Now, as an old woman, I am bewitched by my Permit.

The next day I woke with optimism. At last a day began with sunshine and a light breeze. The boat headed for deeper water. Land was soon in the distance but two-foot rolling waves made standing a little tricky. I was looking for cloudy water: an indicator of where the bottom is stirred up by feeding fish. I was of a mind to give into the thrill of catching a Bonefish. Having caught them before, I expected that there could easily be a group of them so obsessed with their feeding they'd overlook my look-alike crab fly. The barb of my hook was mashed flat, rendering it useless, giving the advantage to the fish and making it more of a challenge for me. I'd have to keep a tight line, allowing no slack. A fish can slip this type of hook with just a simple shake of its head. In general, I found it easy to hook a Bonefish, possibly because there are so many more of them. I think they are more careless in their enthusiastic eating habits. When they are in a feeding frenzy, they aren't selective. However, they swim like the dickens when they feel the prick of the hook. Before one stops, it will have gone 150 feet and will resist my tug to bring it back so I can release it. I cast into the murky water, crossing my fingers that "something" would be interested in my fly… Bonefish, Jack Crevelles, Permit? At the end of the day I had hooked, landed and released two Bonefish and six Yellowtail Snappers. No Permit encountered, I was unable to appreciate my success.

On the last day I thought of other last days, always a time when I'm unable to shake a melancholy mood, overwhelmed by an awareness that I'll be leaving soon. I always want one more day, one last opportunity. Some last days are no different than the previous days, but others are memorable. I knew it was possible that this last day could be the highlight of the trip. Once, in the fading hours in the Seychelles after an exhausting walk across a dry coral flat, I cast mindlessly, almost desperately, into a stream of incoming tide. And after reeling in a thirteen-pound Bonefish, the biggest I had ever seen, I was sure it was my reward for not giving up. So, on this last day, heading for Cayos Los Pájaros, I was optimistic. I didn't give up hope that at the end of the day I would hold my Permit.

Leaving Cayo Lago the next day, I climbed aboard a rickety and deafening Russian helicopter. The noise was disconcerting, disturbing my thoughts of the day before. On my last day in Cuba the weather was perfect—cloudless skies, with winds five to fifteen knots. A beautiful day to be on the water. It was a good day for reflection and sadly, little else.

Hemingway's old man, Santiago, caught his fish, his Marlin, only to see it gradually disappear before his eyes, eaten by sharks. Which is worse … not seeing your fish at all or connecting with your fish and seeing that you have little control over the outcome?

Santiago, what gives meaning to our continuing search? Yes, I know that fishing is your livelihood, but it's also about a challenge isn't it? I think it's integral to who you are—as it is for me. I know what it feels like when everything comes together—the perfect cast, the unexpected hookup and the thrill of the fight. I know how good it is when I get everything right. Yes, there's luck. But I see how quietly you persevere and I admire that. We both understand that sometimes we will fail to achieve that which we worked so hard for. There is some solace in that acceptance. Ah, but those times of unexpected and memorable successes are forever ingrained. We have confronted the fish and nature. Having had that encounter sustains us. I am old with my memories. And like you, I am making plans for the next time.

Carilda Oliver Labra

The Poet, the Poems, the Map, and Matanzas

Joanna Biggar

I go crazy, love, I'm a mess
When I go in your mouth, delayed;
and almost without reason, almost for nothing,
I touch you with the tip of my breast.

From "Me Desordeno, Amor, Me Desordeno"
— Translation by Linda Watanabe McFerrin

It was poetry that would bring me to Matanzas.

As my young friend and guide in Havana recited this verse to me by renowned poet and national treasure, Carilda Oliver Labra, I was astonished. Carilda, as she is universally called, broke barriers and taboos, writing erotic, sensual, revolutionary poetry, and becoming an icon for women's freedom. When her upper-middle-class family fled Cuba for Florida, Carilda stayed behind. After teaching law then art in Havana, she eventually came back to live in her native city of Matanzas, a place my friend urged me to visit. Guidebooks often call it the "Athens of Cuba," a city of poets. Though a bit edgy these days, my friend cautioned, I should go there, and meet Carilda—now ninety-five—who famously opens her door to strangers.

Intrigued, I began haunting Havana's bookstores to find one of her books, but to no avail. Then I tried one of Havana's wifi hotspots with better luck. I learned that she had a dizzying number of awards and publications—including the National Poetry Award in 1950, the National Literary Award in 1997—and that there is a literary prize in her name in Spain. She was notorious for having many husbands and lovers, among them, according to rumor which Carilda denies, Hemingway. I found a version of Carilda's famous "Canto a Fidel" ("I Sing of Fidel"), written in 1957, two years before the Revolution:

> *I'm not going to name the East,*
> *I'm not going to name the Sierra,*
> *I'm not going to name the war…*
> *I'm going to name all of Cuba*
> *I'm going to name Fidel.*

—Translation by Joanna Biggar

School children across Cuba have sung this for years—and still sing it—and on the fortieth anniversary of its publication, Fidel came to Matanzas to pay Carilda homage.

The allure of a door left ajar to the world of an iconic poet and a fabled city was not to be missed. What I couldn't know then was that the doors revealing what I sought would come in the form of pages opening to me later, long after I had left Matanzas.

Soon, along with my husband, friend, and our delightful guide Orlen, I was on my way. As our car made the hour's trip east from Havana to Matanzas, capital city of the bicoastal Matanzas Province, I took in the towns, oil drilling, the hills of virgin forest, the sea; and, reading my guide books and notes, reviewed what I knew of its history: How Spaniards first spotted the rich land with its bay and many rivers in 1508, and how, years later, a group of thirty decided to raid a native settlement. Engaging some fishermen to row them across a river, the Spaniards, weighed down by heavy armor, were instead dumped overboard by the fishermen and drowned. Hence, the name "Matanzas," or "Massacre," became official at the city's founding in 1593.

I also knew that its surrounding land was soon cultivated for coffee and sugar. A flourishing slave trade, the largest in Cuba, brought many riches. By 1859, 104,514 slaves were listed in the census. Along with many free black citizens, this large population contributed to the thriving Afro-Cuban culture for which Matanzas is famous. Its gifts to the country include *danzón*, rumba, mambo and other dance forms sacred to the African-based Santería religion.

The wealth from these exports also nourished another part of the city's history. Rich planters' sons were sent to study abroad and brought back with them a taste for high European culture, one that delighted in grand architecture, art, music and literature.

As we crossed the Yumurí River toward the center of town, we bumped along a rutted, noisy street, smelling of diesel-fueled trucks and bracketed by collapsing curbs. After dashing through traffic to knock on an unappealing door—our *casa particular*—the word "edgy" came to mind. My vision of the "Athens of Cuba" began to fade. I hoped Carilda would help me restore it.

But first I had to find her. That task, it seemed, would fall to a local guide, journalist Arnoldo Mirvabol, who would not only show us local sites outside of Orlen's orbit, but also serve as liaison to Raidel

Hernandez, Carilda's manager and fourth husband—a man half her age. Arnoldo explained all this as we walked toward the pleasant central square, Parque Libertad, where he began his talk by the requisite statue of famous nineteenth-century revolutionary and poet, José Martí—one of the many heroes Carilda celebrated in verse.

Feeling increasingly unprepared to meet her, I pressed Arnoldo for more information. She was tall, blond and green-eyed, he said, beloved by the local people. In fact, she was beloved by the country and especially Cuban women everywhere, although she had fallen out of favor in the 1970s. But these days she drew crowds whenever she appeared. He himself, along with other journalists, had interviewed her.

"Arnoldo," I said, "I can't meet Carilda with so little information. I really need a book."

"Si," he replied, "I promise I will find you one." And he left to see Raidel. Word came back that Carilda was unwell and would perhaps be ready to meet in two hours. That conversation repeated itself until we all understood that the rendezvous was not taking place. I would leave Matanzas without meeting Carilda. All that remained was the book, and Arnoldo said it would take another day to obtain it. By afternoon the next day, I had a well-read copy of *Calzada de Tirry 81*, Carilda's actual address, in hand.

Before departing, I wanted at least to see the building and pay silent homage to the unmet poet inside, so we stopped briefly before the large, pink colonial-style house needing paint. Its big white door remained shut.

Within days, home at my desk, I finally dove into the book. Turning to the Internet, videos and translations, I felt I was finding Carilda at last. Carilda, a bold poet who celebrated female sexuality, sometimes mixed love and eroticism with male and military power. In

"Declaración de Amor" ("Declaration of Love"), during the Cuban Missile Crisis, she wrote:

> *I ask if I'm wise*
> *when I awaken*
> *the danger between his thighs,*
> *or if I'm wrong*
> *when my kisses prepare only a trench*
> *in his throat.*
>
> *I know that war is probable;*
> *especially today*
> *because a red geranium has blossomed open.*
>
> —Translation by Daniela Gioseffi

Carilda, who also found compassion and love in the poverty surrounding her. In "The Boy Who Sells Greens," she wrote:

> *I found you this morning around the courthouse,*
> *and what a blow your unhappy innocence has given me!*
>
> *My heart which was a urn of illusion*
> *is now like wilted greens, like no heart at all. . .*
>
> —Translation by Daniela Gioseffi

Carilda, who pierced to the heart of family love as it played out through separation. She wrote a poem "To My Mother Who Lives in a Letter from Miami," and summed up the pain of recurring exile in "Soil."

> *When my grandmother came*
> *she brought along a bit of Spanish soil,*
> *when my mother left*
> *she took away a bit of Cuban soil.*
> *I won't hold on to any bit of native land:*
> *I want it all*
> *upon my grave.*

—Translation by Ruth Behar

As for her beloved father, she penned a series of sonnets mourning him after death. In the last, number IV, she wrote:

> *Your dentist chair . . . where is it?*
> *Your student violin . . . how does it sound?*
> *You buried pennies in the sand*
> *and gave my mother other names.*
>
> *I keep all your letters and pictures.*
> *In my dream your prostate is cured.*
> *On the floor of the patio, as in my affection,*
> *your last shoes keep walking.*
>
> *I want to see you go beyond the shutter.*
> *Come, ghost; come, my timely angel.*
> *I no longer know what to do, what to say,*
>
> *because I long to take breakfast*
> *with my father, my sage, my almsman,*
> *at 81 Tirrey Avenue.*

—Translation by Joanna Biggar

This last stanza brings me full circle, back to 81 Tirry, and thoughts of Matanzas. I recall Arnoldo speaking of Carilda's great love for her native city, a place that remains a jumble of disconnected impressions to me. So I turn to her celebrated "Canto a Matanzas" for help. As I read through the romantic Spanish and a bad English translation, I see the fragments of my own memories as puzzle pieces and her long poem as a roadmap where I might find and connect them.

She sings of rivers—the Canímar, the Yumurí, the San Juan—and the geography of the city comes into focus. Then there are the districts—Pueblo Nuevo, Bellamar, Versalles—and the landmarks: the cathedral; the green and open valley; the wet docks; the bridges, for which Matanzas is famous. As her city begins to fill in my map, I can see her in it: "a violent cyclone of loneliness" in its streets; a girl going to school and the cinema; a lovesick woman, as she says, going to la calle del Media to buy an illusion. When she says to Matanzas, "I kiss your patios with flowers/your black stevedores/your bridges and your arenas," I conjure them. And when she addresses Matanzas as "a drug in my veins," I feel it.

But my own experiences begin to fill the map, too. When the words Plaza de la Vigía appear, I think of the famous Teatro Sauto, a neoclassical gem built in 1863, and other elegant edifices. We had driven slowly past the theater's inviting arches. It, like many historic buildings, has been closed for years of renovation. But the city's original square gave glimpses of its storied, lost past. I could imagine its terrifying pirates, its carriages parading stylish people when Matanzas was Cuba's cultural capital.

The many faces of Matanzas show themselves, including the ugly ones. In one stanza Carilda speaks of the "yellow story" of the Morrillo. "Yellow" I take to mean stained, and Morrillo (or Castillo de San Severino) was the slave castle we visited, similar to many I had seen when living in West Africa. Except this one, with stunning views of Matanzas Bay, was on the receiving end of slavery, at the center of Cuba's thriving slave trade. The setting, the fortified walls, the forbidding prison doors, the weathered cannons and rusted chains were all familiar. But mostly I remember, as I place the Morrillo on the map, the galleries of the Museum of the Slave Route, opened in 2009, to honor the suffering and celebrate the cultures of the thousands of enslaved Africans who arrived. Displayed in their native clothing, erect and proud before the cruel trade defined them, they show their diversity with drums and baskets, weapons, jewelry, foods and religious customs which mixed together to form the thriving Afro-Cuban culture and Santería religion. I can still hear the drums of the San Lazarus Day rituals on my street in Matanzas.

I read on, finding references to palm trees and beach. Suddenly I am reliving the day when, hot and defeated, we waited to obtain Carilda's book. What we really wanted was the forbidden pleasure of a heralded beach in Varadero, forty kilometers away. Forbidden to Americans for convoluted political reasons, it still tempted. What if we went anyway? With help, we organized a car and went—undetected—passing a perfect day swimming, lounging on white sand, snorkeling and drinking mojitos. I decided that Carilda, who specialized in pushing boundaries, would bless this transgression. Varadero is indelible on my map.

"*Canto a Matanzas*" sings with the names of revolutionaries and artists. Reading them, I am suddenly transported to a walk in full sun by the San Juan River when Arnoldo ducked in the grill gate of a pastel building. We followed him. Inside the Galeria Taller, a magical space emerged. Around us, indifferent to the heat, artists were hard at work creating sculptures, paintings, jewelry, ceramics, glass and tile works. A soporific Matanzas outside suddenly burst into artistic energy inside this spacious work/live gallery. Artist/manager David

Acosta, who speaks excellent English, welcomed us and explained.

The world-acclaimed sculptor Osmány Bettancourt, or Lola, in 2009 took a trash heap and began transforming it into an artist studio and gallery. With space granted by the local government, he and fellow artists restored the building and in 2012 began selling their art, investing their profit back into the studio. They teach children on Saturdays, attract tourists, and show and sell their work abroad. They also bewitch with hospitality, conversation and offers of tea, while visitors watch works in progress emerge, or ogle masterpieces surrounding them. The genius of Cuba—its tradition of creativity—explodes here.

Finally walking through her pages, I feel I can say I have met Carilda. Using her poetry as guide, I have walked her city, its glorious past, its edgy present, and perhaps even glimpsed its future. In May, 2016, in a march against homophobia and transphobia, as the rainbow flag fluttered in Matanzas, crowds cheered gay activist and daughter of President Raúll Castro, Muriela Castro, who joined in. Then Carilda and husband Raidel opened wide the big door of 81 Tirry to welcome them.

Statue of Che Guevara

Deliberating on Che

Linda Watanabe McFerrin

At ease atop a stony plinth rising high above the palms, the massive form of Che Guevara in mid-march—cap at a rakish angle, rifle at his side—dominates the blue stadium of sky that surrounds us. It is so bright out that I have to tent my hand above my eyes in a near salute to see.

I am in Villa Clara, the Cuban province close to the center of the island where the last battle of the Cuban Revolution was fought in 1958 in its capital city, Santa Clara. It is here that the small armies of Camilo Cienfuegos and Che Guevara united to finally overwhelm the forces of a country in chaos, defeating U.S.-backed dictator Fulgencia Batista and precipitating his flight, first to the Dominican Republic and ultimately to Portugal and Spain. Santa Clara is also the site of the Che Guevara Mausoleum, where the remains of Ernesto "Che" Guevara—doctor, soldier, revolutionary, liberator, hero, and "comrade" or "friend"—as his nickname implies—rest today. He shares the tomb with twenty-nine of the men who fought with him in Bolivia around a decade after his momentous Cuban victory.

By that time, 1968, things had changed drastically in Cuba. Che Guevara and Fidel Castro had done the seemingly impossible. They had deposed a tyrant, up-ended a centuries-long class system, sent those capitalizing on the iniquities of that system packing, and permanently and irrevocably altered the Cuban economy. They had redistributed the wealth of a nation, introduced massive land reform, instituted universal education and medical care, and sewn the seeds of equality amongst a "peasant" populace ... along with a dose of death and an ample spray of bullets.

In Cuba for the first time, I have already noted that in politics, art, letters, culture, as well as in private conversations, Che Guevara is widely loved and revered. In a now communist country with deep roots in a Christianity that its leaders have sought to deny, he is part of a trinity—Fidel Castro, Che Guevara, José Martí—that bears a not surprising resemblance to the father-son-holy ghost New Testament threesome. Then there's the whole "healing the lepers" thing.

I guess I should reveal at this point that I actually missed a good deal of the bad press on Che and Castro. Since a substantial portion of my childhood was spent in England and Japan, I was not significantly informed or impacted by the whole Cuban-Missile-Crisis-thing. While other elementary school kids were learning to "duck and cover," I was watching Japanese cartoons about robots and magical beings, celebrating Hinamatsuri (Girls' Day) Koinobori (Boys' or Children's Day), making fans, flying kites, and folding paper cranes. When my grandmother died and I finally returned to the United States, it was to inhale the potent mix of anti-imperialist, anti-Viet Nam, anti-racism, Summer-of-Love fumes that haloed the San Francisco Bay Area ... so I strongly supported every nation's rights to self-determination, especially where the will of the people seemed to be in favor of it. Wrong or right, that's the lens through which I viewed the Cuban Revolution and Che. And this was long before I read *The Motorcycle Diaries* ... and that is where the lepers came in.

Introduced by South American publisher Verso Books in 1995, *The Motorcycle Diaries—Diarios de Motocicleta*—is the personal account of twenty-three-year-old Ernesto "Che" Guevara de la Serna's second youthful travel adventure in 1952. His first, undertaken two years into his medical studies, took him 2800 miles on a motorized bicycle through northern Argentina to San Francisco del Chañar near Cordoba where he met with patients at the leper center run by his friend Alberto Granado. The second adventure—this time along with Alberto on a single-cylinder 500cc Norton that they named *La Poderosa* (the Mighty One)—was much more ambitious. The nine-month motorcycle adventure gradually devolved into a 5,000-mile bus-boat-train-walk-sometimes-even-swim odyssey across South America and beyond.

Although it begins in a mist of romance, in Miramar, Argentina, with a hot-blooded young Ernesto bidding a lengthy romantic farewell to girlfriend Chichina, the diary quickly takes on the irresistible shape of a picaresque chronicle of quixotic encounters. The tone darkens as the landscape and the lives of the people that the two men encounter harden. In Chile Ernesto and Alberto come face to face with the despair and poverty of the men and women who toil away in the hellish conditions of mines run by U.S. monopolies. In Peru they are confronted by the plight of indigenous people brutalized by the expectations and disregard of the proponents of modern civilization. But it is in their work with the lepers in Lima and San Pablo that the most potent and transformative interactions seem to take place.

This is where Ernesto "Che" Guevara de Serna wins me over for good and all. His care and concern for these people of such little hope is deeply moving. In a letter to his father from Iquitos on June 4, 1952, ten days before he turns twenty-four, he writes:

> *The farewell which the patients in the Lima hospital gave us was enough to carry on .... Their appreciation stemmed from the fact that we didn't wear overalls or gloves, that we shook hands with them as we would with the next man, sat with them, chatted about this and that, and played football with them.*
> —Motorcycle Diaries
>   Translation by Ann Wright

And I am with him.

In Santa Clara, in the mausoleum, years after reading those diaries, I study a much more potent rebellion than Che's early pan-American journey. In the photos and text of the exhibits I am introduced to a later Guevara, one who still struggles with the same asthmatic reactions to jungle and dust, the same torment and provocations of conscience. But this life journey takes place under the banner of revolution, and he is no longer merely a witness. This is the Che I had been introduced to, now in a far more toxic form; his allergies and his strengths have become legendary. I am in warrior's tomb, one in which he is celebrated, his victories shrouded in admiration. I search in vain for any dissonant note, find only the information that confirms the perception of him as a hero loved by all.

I return to the sunlit exterior of the mausoleum somewhat shaken.

Later, in Trinidad, where Joanna and I enjoy the culinary, musical and inebriant pleasures of what we are told was once a sleepy little village, we make a trip with our guide into a countryside where a slave and peasant populace once manned the vast sugar plantations. Even in the ruins their anguish is evident. The heat and the remnant squalor of their conditions are a horror bearing down on us.

In Cienfuegos, the beautiful Caribbean port city on Cuba's south central coast, the broad boulevards and graceful neoclassical architecture underscore the old disparity in the fortunes of the Cuban populace. Now a UNESCO World Heritage designated site, it could not stand in more striking contrast to the poor villages that sprout in the other parts of the island. However, it is at the Museo de Playa Girón, the Bay of Pigs war museum, that I get a final piece to the puzzle that Che has become for me.

In the little two-room museum in the Cuban province of Matanzas, I am immersed in the full Cuban perspective on the U.S. government-orchestrated, CIA-funded attack on Fidel Castro and Cuba's increasingly communist government in 1961. It is a David vs. Goliath story that is presented here—a story in which men and women, young and old mostly poor Cubans fight with inferior weapons against the full force of imperialist might. The genesis of the invasion, the duplicitous cloak of misdirection as to its origin is revealed. The Cuban dead are counted and accounted for, named, their stories told. It is a heartbreaking and profoundly affecting statement about the heroism demonstrated in the face of a seemingly hopeless cause and the significance of the victory. In this story, the big guys are the bad guys and losers while the ordinary men, women and children of Cuba are victorious, but at great personal cost.

This is where the price of heroism is paid. It's counted in death—on both sides—and in the way reality thwarts us, converts political success into great loss of life, repaying good intentions with horrific results.

In a section called "As An Afterthought" in the *Motorcycle Diaries*, apparently written by Che once he had returned home from his youthful journey, he remembers a late night conversation with a fellow traveler in an ethereal space under a starry sky. In the course of their dialogue, the fellow says to him:

"The future belongs to the people and gradually or suddenly they will take power, here and all over the world. The problem is ... that the people need to be educated and they can't do that before taking power, only after. They can only learn from their mistakes, and those will be serious and will cost many innocent lives.... Revolution is impersonal, so it will take their lives and even use their memory as an example or as an instrument to control the young people coming after them."

"Despite what he said," writes Guevara, "I now knew ... that when the great guiding spirit cleaves humanity into two antagonistic halves, I will be with the people ... I see myself being sacrificed to the authentic revolution, the great leveler of individual will, pronouncing the exemplary *mea culpa*."

In this, I think, he has the last word.

The author's first time

My First Time
Thomas Harrell

I was a virgin when I went to Cuba.

Oh, I had thought about it. I confess. But, in my prejudice, I had never even touched one, much less put one in my mouth.

But there I was, eight pairs of eyes on me. Expectant.

And it was the middle of the day.

Before Cuba, I thought of cigars like Victorian children: best seen as little as possible; touched rarely; and never smelled. The province of old men, fat and stinky; or worse, the cigars were another toy for extravagant consumption, enjoyed more for status than any inherent pleasure.

Cubans, it is said, are the best. Even for the inexperienced, "Cuban" carries a mystique, an exotic mix of the rare and the forbidden, and until recently spiced with the heady aroma of possible jail time.

The reputation of Cuban cigars is so strong that in 1963 President Kennedy ordered his Press Secretary—and fellow Cuban aficionado—Pierre Salinger out into a cold February night in Washington to collect all the Cuban cigars he could before Kennedy signed the trade embargo. Salinger later said he returned to the White House with 1,200 of the President's favorite Cuban cigars—and moments later,

Kennedy signed the trade embargo.

I'm no Jack Kennedy, I thought, but I could try at least one.

Three hours west of Havana lies Cuba's answer to our "tobacco road," the *ruta tabaco*. Here, in the foothills and mountains of the far west of this long, languid island, the marriage of soil, sun, and rain is ideal for growing tobacco.

Our day in Viñales, the valleys and hills that surround the famous karst mountains of the same name, led us through the green heart of the *ruta tabaco*.

Our timing was perfect. December is the middle of the growing season, dry and warm. Sun is the friend of tobacco; rain the enemy. The leaves highest on the tobacco plant, those that luxuriate longest in the sun—the *ligero*—are the most flavorful. On all sides we could see adolescent tobacco, laid out in neat rows, their broad green leaves waving in the mountain breezes like elephants' ears. Some farms were mere plots of land, tilled and nurtured by hand; others covered several acres and boasted a small truck or even a tractor. Some farms belonged to families; others to the government. Either way, almost all tobacco is sold to the government monopoly to supply the government-owned cigar factories.

Tobacco, like sugar, is critical for the Cuban economy. Both are Cuba's face cards in trade, first with the Soviet Union and now increasingly with China. But only cigars are Cuba's ambassador to the world, known everywhere, welcomed by heads of state. Cigars were a favorite gift from Fidel Castro, an omnipresent introduction to a country and a culture, and a way, perhaps, of making a revolutionary in fatigues a bit more approachable.

Our destination was an organic farm owned by the Ruiz family. The family engages in nascent capitalism by cultivating tobacco, giving tours, and rolling their own cigars for sale to Cuban and foreign tourists. Marco Ruiz met us at the barn where tobacco dries; two lean dogs, at this point unimpressed by Americans, watched us, from the shade of a muddy tractor.

The barn was instantly familiar; it reminded me of my grandparents' barn on the Tennessee farm where I played as a kid. Sunlight filtered through faded boards, the smells of horses and leather and hay pleased the nose. But here, Marco explained, the smell was tobacco. Brown, wrinkled leaves drying from the rafters. Tobacco leaves hand-picked and sorted into piles based on color and age, ready for fermentation. And in a place of honor, a bucket with the family's own special blend of rum, cinnamon, pineapple, and local fruit juices—a quick dip for the cigars before smoking. A unique family recipe, passed through the generations.

Marco explained how a cigar is rolled. It seemed simple enough: five leaves, three for the body of the cigar, to blend strength and flavor; one as a binder; and a half leaf as the wrapper, or "dress." But as math will tell you, five leaves can be combined thirty-two ways—and that is before the leaves are sorted for a dizzying range of color, age and fermentation; each cigar graded for taste, strength, size and flavor.

Not quite so simple.

A short walk away, Marco's cousin Henry was holding court in an open-air pavilion. Whereas Marco had explained the process, Henry actually rolled the brown, mature leaves into the family's blend of a *cohiba*, one of the most prestigious blends and the one most favored by Fidel. Bundles of cigars sat next to Henry, waiting to be sold.

Henry sat behind a semi-circular rough wooden counter. Stocky and solid, he rarely looked down at the leaves in front of him; his hands moved easily from memory. We took our places in front of Henry, waiting in a half-moon like school children, unsure if we were to receive a lesson or a treat. In our case, both.

I was given the place of honor, front and center. My fellow writers watched, their eyes moving from Henry to me and back. Had I made a mistake in revealing my virginity? Yes. Would I be allowed my first time in private? No.

Henry took a fresh cigar and clipped the end so it could be smoked. He dipped the freshly cut end into a small dish of honey.

Henry looked at us. He held up the cigar and used a special lighter to ignite the tip. A butane lighter, or even regular matches, he explained, would affect the delicate flavors of the cigar.

He held out the lit cigar. The tip glowed red. Smoke began to drift. Who would be first?

Everyone looked at me. I nodded, smiled at Henry, and reached for the cigar.

My first Cuban. Rounded. Surprisingly slim; no fat stogy here. Elegant. And a taste of honey.

"Only in the mouth," Henry warned again. "Don't inhale."

I took the cigar from Henry's hand, held it gingerly, and put it to my mouth, a sweet introduction. I tasted the honey. Absurdly, I thought of Mary Poppins: a spoonful of sugar?

I carefully took my first drag. A little at first, careful not to inhale.

The smoke was more mellow than I'd expected. The sweetness of honey to start; a finish of leather, earth, age, and grass. Easy in the mouth.

I exhaled. No embarrassing cough. I smiled at Henry, at my friends, to myself. I sucked again, deeper, more confident. I filled my mouth with the smoke and savored the taste. Exhaled slowly, watching the smoke trail away. No fancy rings, yet … but I was a veteran.

This was something I could enjoy. Would enjoy, again.

But I would always remember my first time.

My curiosity aroused, I wondered if a state-run cigar factory could be anything like the farm.

Luckily, one of Cuba's oldest cigar factories, the Flor de Tabacos de Partagas, was a pleasant half-hour walk from our *casa particular*. Partagas has been in Havana since 1845, and after my tour, I wasn't sure too much had changed in the intervening years.

Forget visions of Henry Ford. Partagas is a factory only in the sense it covers a city block and soars four stories around a grand old atrium. But inside, you hear not the grind and clack of machines, but the steady buzz of hundreds of workers.

Surprisingly, the factory resembles the Ruiz farm in one significant way: All the cigars—up to 20,000 a day—are made individually by hand. While other workers in the factory grade the leaves and select wrappers, hundreds of *torcedores*—the rollers—combine, roll and press the leaves into dozens of different brands, each brand boasting a unique recipe of age, color, flavor, size and strength.

The *torcedores* sit in rows of a dozen or so workers in a cavernous room almost the length of a city block, each with a table and old-fashioned wooden press. Bundles of leaves lie next to each worker, to be combined and rolled in the special recipe unique to the brand assigned to the roller that day. The more experienced the roller, the more expensive the brand he or she makes.

These *torcedores* were mostly young, at least to my eyes, the equivalent of Cuban millennials. They wore jeans and T-shirts and tank tops in the warm, humid, casual atmosphere. They cut, twisted, folded, rolled and pressed the tobacco leaves as they talked, gossiped and listened to the omnipresent *radio-novelas* and music that played throughout the factory. A few smoked the product, apparently a perk of the job.

Many cigar factories still employ *lectores*, readers chosen by the workers to sit at the front of the room, a tradition dating to 1865 and attributed to a crusading journalist determined to educate as well as entertain the *torcedores* during the monotonous work. These *lectores* are even credited with helping fuel the revolution against Spain.

I was not fortunate enough to see or hear a *lectore* that day, but my guide, Augustin, assured me the *lectores* are more likely to read from the official Communist newspaper than from novels these days, tempering my disappointment. But literature plays an important part in the cigar mystique—the famous Cuban brands *Romeo y Julieta* and *Montecristo* are said to have been inspired by favorite books.

Despite the hint of mystery and romance, the reality of socialism is not far away. Every worker has the same quota of 110-120 cigars a day, and everyone is paid the same—the equivalent of about forty U.S. dollars a month. There is no incentive to produce more, and most workers leave by mid-afternoon.

It seems a benign—even generous—policy, but every cigar factory is owned by the government, so there is no way to seek better pay or conditions, or to advance based on effort or creativity.

And the work is hard. After fifteen to twenty years of the repetitive work, many rollers are crippled by carpal tunnel syndrome or other ailments related to tobacco exposure. This might explain the youth of the *torcedores*. And their inevitable "retirement" is the Cuban social safety net, increasingly threadbare.

As I think about it, I can't decide if the casual dress, flexible schedule and absence of Darwinian competition is a humane contrast to the more "advanced" tech-heavy, rigid, increasingly robotized factories of the affluent West, or simply a way to turn necessity into a virtue: cheap human labor as a substitute for more efficient, and potentially safer—but unaffordable—machinery.

Before Cuba, I never gave cigars much thought. And what thoughts I gave were negative. Now, I have a stash of *cohibas*, organic and "artisanal" of course, waiting at home. And, for better or worse, they are perfectly legal. No need for a late-night run in the snow.

I'm glad my first time was among friends, on a family farm, on a warm afternoon. The memory will be with me always when I indulge in a Cuban, a sweetness even absent the honey.

But I will think, too, of the thousands of young Cuban men and women who toil to make the cigars enjoyed by presidents and millionaires, with little to show for it. Cigars are a potent symbol of Cuba: a cultural and historical icon; an indelible link to Fidel and revolution; and proof of Cuban resilience.

But symbols are rarely untarnished. Behind the smoke lies another truth: the work is still hard, the pay is still low, the physical toll is still high, the cost of good cigars still out of reach for cigar workers and ordinary Cubans alike. Even in a socialist paradise, the more things change, the more some things remain the same.

Preparing for dinner at Paladar Los Mercaderes

Cuba—Full of Flavor
Laurie McAndish King

Pretty much all I knew about Cuba before I visited was that it was one of the last bastions of communism and the home of passionate revolutionaries, photogenic old American cars and tasty pork sandwiches. The rest was a mystery.

So I didn't know what to expect when I visited the organic farm and restaurant in Viñales, a lush agricultural area about 100 miles southwest of Havana. Standing at the entrance, I flicked the farm's business card with my thumbnail and considered its claim. The card said, in bold aqua-colored letters, "*El Paraiso.*" The Paradise. It was followed by another line in smaller type: "*Una Pasion Natural.*" A Natural Passion. This farm tour I'd signed up for was going to be fun.

The early December sun was warm on my back as I looked out over long green rows of lettuce, Swiss chard, onion, cabbage, carrots, radishes and peppers poking up from the brown soil at El Paraiso. Honey bees buzzed at the red torch ginger and orange marigolds that brightened a winding pathway. In the distance, flat sugarcane fields morphed into clusters of craggy pine-tree-covered hills that looked like slumbering dragons.

"We have thirteen hectares," our guide, Marilyn, said, "and everything we serve is grown here except the fish." Marilyn was tall and slender and wore a bright yellow top that matched her sunny disposition. Even though English was her second language, she spoke it very well—and, like most Cubans, very quickly. I struggled to keep up.

"Twenty percent of what we produce is sold to the government and is then distributed—for free—to a small hospital and a primary school," Marilyn continued. "We are biodynamic and organic. We don't use any chemicals."

"How do you deal with the insects?"

"We plant marigolds with the corn," she explained. "Our oregano, onions, and three kinds of basil help, too." We followed the path to a section where lettuce was sprouting. I smelled mint and anise as my bare legs brushed against wayward plants.

"Sticky traps, like these, help too." Marilyn pointed to index-card-sized pieces of colored paper interspersed with the lettuce. "Tropical insects love yellow; those traps catch fifty percent of the insects. The white and blue sticky traps catch twenty-five percent each.

"We grow banana, plantain, cashews, strawberries, spinach, and celery. Sugar cane is used for rum and *guarapo*—that's an aphrodisiac." Marilyn mentioned this matter-of-factly. Hmmm. Was *guarapo* the key to El Paraiso's "natural passion?" I wondered whether it was included with the hospital and school provisions, but Marilyn didn't give me time to ask.

"We get wood from the forest and use a spring pump for irrigation. Kitchen waste goes to compost, and so do ashes from cooking charcoal," she continued. Marilyn covered a lot of ground. "The rabbits' dung is used for fertilizer: Earthworms process it, and then we combine it with compost. We feed the rabbits sweet potatoes. Honey, coriander, chickens, geese ..." she could have gone on, but I was ready to sample the cuisine so I ambled over to a shaded picnic table and grabbed a seat near some of the other visitors.

Where to begin? A sign on the wall recommended the anti-stress drink El Paraiso was famous for, and even provided the recipe:

Cóctel Antiestrés

Jugo de Piña
1 Hojita de Anís
1 Hojita de Menta
1 Hojita de Hierba Buena
1 Hojita de Albahaca
1 Hojita de Caña Santa
Una Pizca del Leche de Coco
Miel
Canela
Ron opcional

Carlos, our server, brought out tall glasses of the frothy beverage, and translated the list of contents: pineapple juice, anise, spearmint, yerba buena, basil, lemongrass, coconut milk, honey and cinnamon. I tried to remember—were any of those potent anti-stress ingredients? The rum, or *ron*, was probably important if one wanted to experience the full anti-stress effect, but my drink didn't taste alcoholic.

The explanation emerged when Carlos returned holding up what looked, from a distance, like a bottle of rum. "This is *Vitamin R*," he explained solemnly. "*R* is for rum. Officially optional, but it helps with the stress."

Ah-ha! Another clue to that natural passion, I thought, as everyone at the table poured liberally from the bottle of Vitamin R.

The published recipe for Cóctel Antiestrés doesn't reveal all of the beverage's ingredients. When I asked whether the drink was dairy-free, Carlos said no, and brought me a slightly less-foamy version. And I tasted nutmeg, which hadn't been disclosed as an ingredient. But I didn't stress out about it—I couldn't, really. After all, I was in Paradise. And the Vitamin R was flowing freely.

Next up was the organic, biodynamic, chemical-free meal. It was served family-style: crispy mounds of hand-sized taro and cassava chips, a fabulous soup, platters of chicken, delicate fish, tender pork, sweet potato, pumpkin, lettuces, crunchy pickled vegetables, and rice with beans. Silence descended on the table as we scooped up one delicious mouthful after another. Aromatic steam rose from the thick yellow soup. It was full of chunks of sweet vegetables, bursting with flavor. I had to have the recipe.

"Carlos, this soup is delicious. Do you think you could get me the recipe?" I asked boldly, perhaps inspired by the Vitamin R.

Moments later Olga Lidia, the chef and a co-founder of the farm, appeared. Olga had chocolate-colored skin, friendly crinkles around her eyes, and a big smile. Her aqua T-shirt sparkled with hundreds of sequins. She wrote for me in a large, loopy script:

Zanahoria, rábano, pepino, habichuela, malonga, calabaza, col, ajo, cebolla, ají, pimiento, comieno, pimienta (al gusto), aceite, bijol

I assumed it was a list of the ingredients for the soup. "That's a lot of vegetables—and you grow them all here?"

"Yes, so many vegetarians came to the restaurant," Olga explained in Spanish as Carlos translated. "I created this recipe especially for them. But the soup is better—*muy rico*," she added with a wink, "if you include beef, pork, or chicken. It's best with all three." Olga's recipe and methodology—translated below—are simple:

> Carrot, radish, cucumber, kidney beans, taro, pumpkin, cabbage, garlic, onion, red pepper, bell pepper, cumin, black pepper (to taste), oil, annatto
>
> Cook all together until the flavor is right.
> Serve warm.
> Enjoy!
>
> Chef Olga Lidia
> Founder of the Farm

Cuban food, I had learned, is much more than pork sandwiches. El Paraiso gave me a good perspective on the first half of the country's farm-to-table arrangement: small-scale growing, companion planting and integrated pest management. Now it was time to visit a *paladar* —one of Cuba's privately owned restaurants, which are often in the homes of their owners.

I felt a little guilty, because most local people can't afford to eat in *paladars*. Unless they're pulling in foreign money from the tourism industry, Cubans eat mainly rice and beans, with occasional chicken or pork for protein. But *paladars* are the appropriate place for tourists to eat, and I resolved to infuse money into the country by dining at as many as possible.

"You must visit Paladar Los Mercaderes," my fellow traveler Linda insisted after we'd been in Havana a few days. "The staircase leading up to the restaurant is lined with rose petals. And the owner, Yamil, is *very* handsome." Linda smiled conspiratorially, and I began planning my visit immediately.

When I arrived at Paladar Los Mercaderes, the first thing I saw was a white marble staircase with flickering votive candles and—just as Linda had described them—velvety red rose petals sprinkled on every step, drawing me upwards. I half expected to see sexy lingerie and abandoned shoes scattered at the top. Was there "natural passion" at Cuban *paladars*, as well as at the farms? What if I'd come at the wrong time of day, and caught someone *in flagrante delicto*? This *was* in someone's home, after all.

Yamil stood at the top of the stairs. "Hello, Laurie. Nice to meet you." Yes, he was handsome, with glossy hair and twinkly eyes. And he was fully clothed.

"Yamil! Good to meet you. Thanks for taking the time to talk with me. I have to ask the obvious question first. The entrance is so romantic. What's the story of all these rose petals?"

"Well, I will tell you," Yamil said, speaking softly as we sat down at a table near the bar. I had to lean forward to hear him over clatter and conversation coming from the kitchen. It turned out this was a habit of Yamil's, and every time he lowered his voice and said, *Well, I will tell you,* I leaned forward and listened intently.

"I said to my wife, 'Why don't we try to make a restaurant where we would like to go?' And we definitely would love to walk up stairs with rose petals and candles welcoming us. So that is why, since we opened five years ago, every single day we have rose petals—not only on the stairs, but also on the toilet—even when people told us we were crazy to spend the money."

"I'm glad you did; you've created a beautiful restaurant," I observed. Art hung on every wall and chandeliers glowed beneath high ceilings. Red tablecloths and sparkling dinnerware enhanced the romantic feeling. Three giant windows each opened onto their own small balcony with a private table overlooking the street. Live Afro-Cuban music drifted in on a warm breeze. I began to wish I'd brought my own handsome man along.

"And then our dream started, like that." Yamil continued, interrupting my reverie. "This room where we are sitting now, this was our daughter's room. And that was our bedroom. Look at tiles on the floor; you can see where a wall used to be."

I tried to imagine the space as a home, and wondered what the bedrooms might have looked like, but aromas wafting from the kitchen made it impossible to think of anything but food. "What kind of cuisine do you serve?"

"Seafood, pork, chicken. My wife and I are very picky about food. We focus on bringing the best recipes of the countryside to our menu. When the Spanish came to Cuba, they brought African people, who brought spicy food. My wife's favorite is the spicy seafood dish with fish, shrimp, lobster, and octopus."

Salivating, I asked, "What spices do you use?"

"Well, I will tell you," Yamil said. I leaned in closer. "Cumin, curcumin, oregano ... and we use, of course, very good garlic. It's not as big as the one I see in some other countries, but the taste is just amazing. We were forced to be organic before that became fashionable. Now people appreciate that when the food is organic, it's more healthy, you know? Our black beans are very creamy. We call them *frijoles negros dormidos*."

"*Dormidos?*" I thought Yamil had said *creamy*, but maybe I misunderstood. I leaned in even closer.

"That would be like sleeping black beans, because they are very creamy," he said. "When you look at the black beans, they look like they are sleeping."

Sleeping black beans? Because they are creamy? There was some part of this metaphor—something about the combination of sleeping and creamy—that was lost in translation. Yamil didn't give me a chance to dive into the etymology, though.

"They are exquisite!" he continued enthusiastically. "But these black beans are almost impossible to find in the market, so we went to the countryside to find a family farming them. We do the same with lamb; we have an old man who is feeding them in the natural way. They benefit with us, and we are very happy working with them. This is a winning-winning relationship."

Then Yamil lowered his voice again, as if he were about to divulge a secret. "I will tell you. Happy animals walking free—that makes the quality of the meat very different. With our pork, too, it's from just one family in a small little town."

"What's *your* favorite Cuban food?"

"Me? Definitely, I love pork. It is always on the menu of Cuban people. It's especially good when fed with little coconuts—the fruit of the royal palm tree, *palmiche*. Countryside people discovered this by accident: When they had open cages by the royal palm tree, the flavor is just *amazing*."

"You sound so passionate when you talk about food, Yamil...."

"Yes, well we were very happy when Obama opened possibilities for Americans to visit Cuba, but now we are dramatically affected by new regulations of the United States government. I have a lot of friends who are trying to survive this crisis of having almost no tourism. I believe that if people outside Cuba know how good our food is they will decide to come here one day, and that definitely will help the people. As we say, *We are relatives, we are neighbors, and we love each other.*"

Most of Cuba is still a mystery. I didn't meet any revolutionaries while I was there, and although they do use a home-grown aphrodisiac, I didn't figure out whether it really was a paradise. But

I did develop a neighborly love for the country, its inhabitants and their cuisine. Cuba is, as Yamil would say, *full of flavor*. Next time I visit it will be with a full heart, an empty stomach—and my own handsome companion.

Havana streets feel safe at night

BEHIND CLOSED DOORS

Christine Berardo

I was a junior in college the day the door to Cuba slammed shut. We were on the brink of thermonuclear war: Soviet ships loaded with nuclear missiles were steaming toward launch pads ninety miles off our shore; President Kennedy was sending the U.S. Navy to intercept them. I was nineteen and the world was about to end. I stepped from class into a beautiful fall day in Southern California, the professor's last words ricocheting in my head: "We'll continue Thursday, if we're all still here."

We were. A week later the crisis was over and we moved on with the Cold War. Cuba was put in the deep freeze and declared off limits to U.S. travelers. But I get a little crazy about doors that say "Do Not Enter." What's on the other side? Like Eve in the garden, I began to wonder, as time went by, if I was being protected from something or denied a delicious tropical fruit. So decades later, when the chance to go to Cuba with a group of writers comes my way, I quickly sign up.

We are staying in Casa Dalia, a *casa particular* in Old Havana. I've seen two women, an old man, a boy, and a small dog that wanders out from time to time. They come and go, disappearing behind a low wrought-iron gate at the end of a catwalk-like balcony that connects the rooms along the courtyard. They enter a small door nearly obscured by the sheets, towels, underwear and boys' pants drying on lines that take up the entire end balcony, but for the rocking chair where the old man sits during the day.

Whenever I'm in a strange place, I hunger to make personal contact, to move past the barriers of separation. Perhaps it has to do with growing up in a Lutheran parsonage where my father never failed to welcome any and all strangers who came to our door. So I want to know how this family lives, to enter their world. I want to know what's behind the door.

The younger woman, probably in her forties, is Dalia. Each morning Dalia or her mother, Teresa, the *casa's* owner, sets a tall pitcher of frothy freshly-made pineapple juice on the table, along with a plate of fresh tropical fruit, a thermos of excellent strong Cuban coffee and another of hot milk, and a plate of *bolillos*. The cold, sweet juice is so delicious it could be my forbidden fruit. How does she make it? "*Cómo se hace?*" I ask Teresa in my limited Spanish. "*Por máquina o a mano?*"

I ask because I am curious. About more than the juice. I want to see her kitchen. I am trying to piece together a picture of her life. She says she is happy to work. By which I understand she is grateful to be in the private economy, able to earn much more changing sheets and cleaning toilets for guests than, say, a doctor with a government salary equivalent to about thirty dollars a month. I assume renting rooms is the sole source of income for Teresa and her daughter. But what did she do before she inherited the house that was once the home of her Spanish grandfather? While I was in the streets in the '70s protesting the Vietnam War, was she a revolutionary loyal to Fidel? I am searching for common footing. Where was she in October of 1962?

Did she even know? Were ordinary Cubans told about the impending peril just off their shore? Curious about how Teresa might have experienced that harrowing moment in time, I am soon following a path that leads me to a sign on the lush lawns of the Hotel Nacional: *EXHIBITION ON THE MISSILE CRISIS (1962)—TRENCHES AND BUNKER*. I am stopped at another closed door. This one of iron and below ground. I join a tour and discover it leads to an underground bunker, and from there through open trenches to a twisting warren of tunnels. These defenses were built in 1961 to protect Cuba from future invasion from *el Norte* after the CIA-led Bay of Pigs attack that convinced Fidel to allow Soviet missiles on his soil.

I enter the dark tunnel. I have to stoop to avoid bumping my head on overhead rocks. The narrow passage is claustrophobic, the air stifling. The same airless feeling, sandwiched here among strangers, that I felt that terrible day when I stumbled numb and stupefied from class to await the evening news.

Returning to the bunker, I stop at a photo of a mom holding a child with a tin bucket on her head. It could be Teresa with her little Dalia. The words on the toddler's bucket-hat read, "*MI PAPA ESTA EN LA TRINCHERA*" ("my daddy is in the trench"). Make-believe protection from the "if-we're-all-still-here" catastrophe.

One morning back in the casa, Teresa allows me to follow her into her tiny kitchen to see the *máquina eléctrica* in which the juice is made. I'd imagined some fancy contraption but it's just an old blender. In rapid-fire Cuban Spanish she explains how she turns a fresh pineapple into juice. I pretend to understand while glancing around the kitchen. It is the size of a walk-in pantry. How does she manage? The sink is piled high with the breakfast dishes of her guests. A refrigerator like one my mother had in the '50s just fits in a small alcove off the kitchen. A washing machine fills another nook. Teresa indicates two closed doors, one to her bedroom, the other to the room shared by her sixteen- and nineteen-year-old grandsons. This seems to be the extent of the family's living space. No evidence of a table to eat at or a couch to sit on. What kind of family life is possible in such cramped conditions?

"Dalia and I work," Teresa tells me matter-of-factly. "The boys study." The old man I've seen hanging around is her ex-husband. "*Él es mi amigo, pero no en la cama,*" she confides with a grin. They are friends, but not in bed.

We return to Teresa's large airy *sala* that fronts on the street below. The mismatched decor appears chosen from dregs left behind when someone left for Miami or died. A large painting of blue sky and billowy white clouds dominates one wall. On another, an adolescent boy stares dewy-eyed from a colossal color photo, his ringed fingers pressed together at his lips in the pose of a Santería Initiate immersed in water to his shoulders. A crucifix overlooks the breakfast table, where snowmen in red and green mufflers frolic across the tablecloth. Christmas—in officially atheist communist Havana? I would ask Teresa about the apparent theological contradictions here but am thwarted by the limits of my conversational Spanish.

She wants me to meet Abran, her schoolboy grandson. *"Como el presidente, Abran Lincoln."* When he comes in from school, she introduces us. I recognize the face: He is the Santería boy on the wall.

As twilight falls in Habana Vieja, people pour into the narrow streets. I step into the river of bodies on the way to bars and cafés or heading home. Silky tropical air caresses my skin. Knots of young people perch on walls and cluster in courtyards around hotspots, their fingers furiously tapping cell phones as they vie to get online.

"We love you guys!" a man shouts, "but we don't want another war." He has noticed Obama's image on my tote bag. Barack Obama is a hero here, ever since his 2016 visit, the first U.S. President to set foot in Cuba since 1928. Ever since, he cracked open the door. Now, two years later, another U.S. President is trying to close it again.

Electricity is not to be squandered on neon signs or gratuitous illumination. Darkened buildings loom above, their ruined facades romantic in shadow. Overhead, a silvery moon plays peek-a-boo with lacy clouds. I am surprised by how safe it feels walking in the dark among strangers. A sexy and mysterious sense of anything-can-happen in the amber half-light of occasional streetlamps. Plunging necklines and ass-hugging shorts reveal abundant bare flesh, ranging in shade from *café au lait* to ebony. Intoxicating music spills from open windows and doorways, undoing my hips, luring my feet into seductive rhythms.

I always wanted my father to teach me to dance. He said he didn't know how. I didn't believe him. He'd taught me to grow tomatoes, to bait a hook, to bat left-handed. He knew how to dance. But my budding sexuality alarmed him. He was a minister and dancing was a temptation. Tall and awkward, I stood by the wall at school dances and watched my friends who knew all the moves from their dads.

I remember this while sipping mojitos at Café Taberna, where elderly musicians—think Buena Vista Social Club—charm a crowded roomful of tourists. My eyes are riveted on the dance pair, shoulders shimmying, hips gyrating, bodies thrusting and weaving to the music. The man is attractive, fitting compactly into his white shirt and slim-fitting pants, a fedora cocked just-so over trim dark hair and black eyes. I study his moves, how he holds his upper body still while his hips and pelvis swivel suggestively.

Suddenly, as in a dream, fedora man is dancing toward our table, hand outstretched. The woman in front of me refuses with a shake of her head. He shifts his eyes to me, wiggling a finger in invitation. I feel myself rising from my chair, moving toward the floor. I watch him, trying to mirror his moves. My feet move. My ass wiggles. The music enters my bloodstream, banishing inhibition. I giggle, imagining daddy's blush.

It is time to go. As I pack for home, I empty my Obama tote bag and give it to Teresa, a token of our new friendship. She beams, delighted. At the door she has something for me: a business card. It makes me wonder: *Does she see me as a friend or a business opportunity?*

By now my head is swimming. My efforts to connect with people behind the door have brought me face to face with my own ignorance. Are all the smiles merely in the service of getting five stars on Yelp? Is Christmas merely a show put on for tourists? I am like the child in the photo, smiling into the camera, oblivious to the sharks in the water, the nuclear missiles on the ships, the spy planes overhead. She is wearing a bucket on her head. Look, Mommy, isn't this funny?

What I have learned is that what I view as contradiction, Cubans accept as ambiguity. In ambiguity, contradictions are embraced; there's room for situations to be understood in more than one way. To Teresa, both answers can be true.

Everyone here seems to have a double life. Like Javier, the taxi driver who, it turns out, is really a journalist. I see the Cubans I have met as beautiful, warm and friendly. But also careful. They tell me what I want to hear. They seem to know more about me than I do about them. They are watching for any clues I may give off. This is a fine art in Cuba. This is what it is to live in the shadow of state security, not knowing if you are who you represent yourself to be.

I remind myself that long-term trust is not built in a week. In Cuba, it may take years.

I am in awe of the Cubans' perseverance, their resilience, their ingenuity. Their pride in survival. The joy that insists on breaking through. Maybe ambiguity is part of the romance.

Not that ambiguity is unique to Cuba. The father who taught me to connect was afraid to teach me to dance.

Fishermen along the Malecón

My Malecón
Sandra Bracken

My Malecón. That's the way I think about it, this esplanade at the edge of the city by the water. It's possible that the people I see here every day feel the same even if they aren't aware of it.

The fishermen claim their places early every morning. Always engrossed in their casting and conversations; always having a good time (or so it seems), they infuse the morning with optimism, with gusto. Their claim on the Malecón is obvious.

I wake every morning knowing where my first steps will take me. Walking from my *casa particular* through Old Havana on a different route every day ... so easy to get lost. I see José Martí atop his steed facing my destination, the Malecón, say *¡Buenos días!* and thank him for pointing the way. What is it about the water? It holds my first memory of Havana. Seduced by the water and the moment, my husband and I stood briefly hand-in-hand by the seawall in the glow of a setting sun on a balmy evening in June. So unexpected, that moment of intimacy, after a tiring, lengthy day of travel. When we had only a few hours before traveling on, we chose to wander to the waterfront. Perhaps it's no surprise that returning alone I am lured here by the warmth of a memory. And the water. The painting in my head is slightly changed.

Beyond the seawall, a cloudless sky meets the ocean. The different colors of blue are surprisingly pale variations of a slate blue. The horizon is near the bottom of the canvas. Almost imperceptible, steady gentle waves are not interrupted until reaching the rocks at the base of the wall. No ships. No small boats. No drama here today, just the lapping, slapping of water below on the other side of the wall.

Where am I exactly? Does this body of water have a name? Am I looking at the Bay of Havana? Or the Straits of Florida and ninety-three miles to the Florida Keys? The jolt of that thought pulls me out of my reverie to life on this side of the sea wall—to early morning joggers, walkers and people waiting for a ride. Every morning I see that scene repeat itself. It seems that the curb lane of the six-lane roadway is slow-moving to allow for cars to stop momentarily with minimal interference to pick up passengers. Other regulars on the sidewalk are the same two street sweepers. I feel like I know them, though neither has acknowledged me. Except, one morning while waiting for one of them to finish sweeping the area I wanted to walk through, I stood with my back against the wall and noticed a sudden smile on his face just as I was soaked by an errant wave.

Something he knew and I didn't. I laughed in agreement, then wondered what it was like during the recent hurricane. Seeing the sea so docile today, it's hard to imagine waves fourteen feet high crashing easily over the wall, rushing into neighborhoods more than a mile inland.

I confess that when I first imagined this "promenade," I expected tree-lined grassy areas with benches, or perhaps a more tropical, restful, inviting environment—not a wide sidewalk enclosed by a low cement wall on one side, and on the other a very busy highway. I found the deterioration in some areas off-putting at first: deep holes in the sidewalk and crumbling walls. Yet, despite my initial disappointment, this walk has opened me up to seeing Havana from a very particular perspective: It's unusual for me to feel so connected when visiting a new place. I wonder if it's not more inviting to everyone because of its ordinariness. Everyone feels a bit of ownership. Perhaps that's why I feel like it's mine. Everyone can claim a space. It's a place for privacy if you want it ... simply turn your back on the city. Sit on the wall for hours. Sunbathe if you want. Daydream. Meditate. Go blank.

It has always been my habit when traveling to a new place to walk its streets, to get to know it from ground level. But here, I have favored a singular routine, gravitated to the same place over and over ... intuitively. And the city has come to me. If I choose to look toward the road, there's a constant parade of old cars, the pride of many who live here. What if I lived here? Would I always be looking out to sea as I do now? Turning around, looking into the city across the six-lane roadway I see a scene that's hard for me to witness—dilapidated buildings that seem to defy gravity. I feel sad for their shattered beauty. I am attracted to one in particular—the one with caryatids, stately stone women holding up the roof. It's bizarre and beautiful all at once. On one hand, I want to understand why there are so many structures in disrepair, but I am ignorant of their history. I hope for their future. Some have been restored and some wear a second skin of scaffolding. On a corner where I cross over most days, cranes and construction are hidden behind temporary walls.

Can I call it "my Malecón" if I haven't walked the full four miles of it, from the neighborhood of Vedado to the old city, the colonial center, my neighborhood? After taking a taxi to Vedado, I walk west passing few people; here it feels deserted. I notice a towering monument dedicated to the victims of the sinking of the USS Maine during the Spanish-American War—a time when Cuba and the

United States were "friends." When I pass the well-known Hotel Nacional, on a hill across the road, I estimate I have walked two miles, or half the distance. I remember an afternoon on the lawn there, feeling disconnected from the more familiar world below. In late afternoon, I see people I don't see in the morning. Couples. Eyes only for each other or gazing quietly out to sea. Sometimes walking, arms entwined. Or sitting on the wall bodies entwined. I try not to think how much I miss my husband. We would pause to listen to men playing their guitars: but I don't stop. I see an attractive young woman, long dark hair curling around her shoulders, impeccable makeup, cute short gathered skirt. She's by herself, standing seductively by the edge of the roadway. I was told it's a different scene here at night; festive, a younger crowd, lively music—a party scene. One that I won't see. Or hear.

It's getting dark as I approach Castillo de San Salvador and the street where, sadly, I cross into Old Havana one last time. I say ¡*Hasta la próxima vez!* to José Martí. But I have a book of his poems as a remembrance. My Malecón has lured me into a surprising relationship with Havana. My melancholy is tempered with the thought of how easily I will be able to place myself anywhere on the Malecón again, no matter where I am.

Woman in doorway, in Old Havana

Behind the Façade
Tania Amochaev

Habana Vieja, Old Havana, you feed my never-ending search for hidden spaces as few others can. Dark doorways, decaying bricks, broken tiles, moldy corners: I am seduced. I roam behind your collapsing walls, your arched doorways. I cross the thresholds of mystery and climb stairs that lead into darkness to learn your ruins are not abandoned. They surge with life.

Why do your crumbling relics entice me? Why do I abandon inhibitions and invade spaces others would hesitate to enter? What am I looking for? Who am I seeking?

I walk the streets of a city where many buildings are virtually crumbling onto themselves. A city that, in the end, is the product of a revolution gone wrong—a revolution that holds a key to my connection with this place.

The twentieth was a century of revolutions. Deeply resonant to me are the Russian Revolution, the Yugoslavian Revolution, and finally the Cuban Revolution, the one that still survives. All sought to overthrow governments that fostered inequality. All were followed by dictatorships. Two of them had very personal consequences for my family.

My father fled the Russian Revolution as a child, grew up in Serbia, and then was exiled from that seemingly safe haven after the Yugoslavian Revolution, when I was an infant.

Because he was forced to flee, I spent my young childhood in a refugee camp, and the rest of my life in the United States of America. My father regretted his forced flight almost as much as I thanked the universe that we landed in a country that gave me the opportunity to succeed beyond any of his expectations. An opportunity—as I learned over the years—not available to my family who remained in the old country.

Now I was roaming through the consequences of that third revolution in Habana Vieja. Consequences that inevitably brought to mind my memories of visiting Russia and Yugoslavia during those Communist years. Consequences that made me consider how different my life would have been had my father not been forced to flee.

I was searching for what lay inside the destroyed façades. Again and again I walked through a neighborhood of increasingly familiar street scenes. Faded blue, green and cream walls of period buildings; people sitting and chatting on doorsteps; aromas announcing fresh bread hawkers; ropes lifting produce to old ladies on dangerously aging little balconies. On the third day, instead of moving past doorways I had previously eyed with cautious reserve, I followed some instinct that tugged relentlessly at me.

Trepidation accompanied me across the first arched threshold. To my right, beyond that entrance, another crumbling arch opened onto the courtyard of this broken building, into a space filled with abandoned furniture and hanging clothes. To my left, a once-grand staircase rose into the unknown. I silently inched my way back towards the destruction inside the arch.

Just as I had intruded beyond escape, I heard footsteps speeding down the staircase. I froze in place and gazed, mesmerized, as glowing dark skin flashed from the darkness and a large man flew toward me. Before I had a chance to improvise, he caught my eye and paused, startled.

The rebuke I feared never materialized. Instead, he smiled, wished me a *buen día*, a good day, and ran out the doorway. A woman then entered from the street with a loaf of bread. Her eyes were unperturbed as they met mine, and she walked past me through that crumbling courtyard to a tiny doorway under the stairs, a doorway that couldn't possibly lead to a habitation, but did.

It was the first of many such experiences. A little further along that street I explored what was once a grand seven-story palace but now brought to mind images of war-torn cities. The grandeur wasn't fading so much as collapsing and being saved from total destruction by makeshift measures. Old walls of amber and remnants of stained glass glowed onto bare boards and fraying wires strung in random patterns. The original open architecture was accentuated by gaping holes that eliminated all notions of privacy.

In a hidden corner on the third floor, Estrella—a middle aged woman with glowing frizzed red hair—responded to my smile and my extended hand by casually introducing herself and then inviting me in for coffee. Her husband Mario sat in a room the size of many a walk-in closet. We snuggled on the three little chairs that barely fit—mine halfway under the sink as a tiny TV played in the background. I turned down the offer of coffee in my broken Spanish and told them my breakfast awaited me in my *casa particular*, the term for a private home operating as a bed-and-breakfast in Cuba.

On my way out of the building I couldn't resist climbing cautiously up to the next level. Moments later, I briefly saw my new friends—

back in their chairs across the open central courtyard—through a hole in another crumbling wall that seemed a nudge short of total collapse.

Ferocious barking exploded from above, breaking the utter silence. A large dog burst out, snarling, lunging and retreating. The noise escalated, reverberating through the cavernous openings. Memories of being bitten in Cuzco a few years earlier paralyzed me. I knew his jaws would re-open the scar on my calf if I were to turn and flee, but what was my alternative?

I held his eyes as I slowly backed downward, but my fear was energizing him and the sound level grew. Suddenly, Estrella's shout penetrated the din. The dog cowered and backed off, and then his owner emerged to calm him. He and Estrella—clearly good friends—chatted briefly, and peace was restored.

"Take more photographs," Estrella said as she leaned through another opening on the way back to her room, having effortlessly disposed of the danger. "Please!"

I pointed the camera up at her for a final image. We exchanged a few more phrases, and when I wished her luck, she beamed and wished me the same. I noted her address, along Habana Street, and vowed to return the next day.

The dog was quickly forgotten but the exchange between the neighbors stayed with me as I walked back toward breakfast. Tight quarters, open doors, windows lacking glass, no privacy—life lived in the public square. These people might as well have been trapped in an enormous traffic jam for the last sixty years, but there was no road rage on exhibit. Instead, there was a warmth and mutual regard that let them smile openly when a complete stranger entered their world.

It was the kind of warmth that my father missed for years after he fled his Belgrade of the 1950s, around the same era that Havana was still trapped in today. He bemoaned his morning bus rides to work in San Francisco, where passengers kept to themselves. How, he wondered, could they see the same faces daily and yet remain strangers? Where was the warmth and jocularity he so craved?

I didn't really understand, as a child, what it was that he so missed. Why, I wondered, couldn't he just fit in? Why couldn't he be like other fathers? But these people in Havana, with their lives lived in a public square, were tugging at those memories and connecting environments—separated by years and continents—yet mirroring each other. Perhaps San Francisco felt as foreign to him as this environment did to me.

Later that day, I entered another narrow open courtyard. A woman I smiled at along the street had responded by reaching out to me. She noticed my friend Linda, then pointed at herself. Soon we were all weaving back to her rooms, as she repeated "*Chino,*" and pointed to a portrait of her father, hanging in the upper corner, the same spot filled in my father's living room by an Orthodox icon. Her father was handsome and might have been part Chinese. It wasn't all that obvious, but it was clearly a heritage she was proud of.

We returned a few days later to reconnect with her. We learned to spell her name—Carlixta Hernandez—from her ration booklet, as she did not know how to read or write. She still used that ration book—thirty years after the death of the Soviet Union, whose version it was modeled on—to get the rice, beans and cooking oil that supplemented her fifteen-dollar monthly pension.

And again, I started thinking and comparing. I looked around and imagined Yugoslavia as it must have been during my youth, the old country my father couldn't stop missing as I grew to adulthood in my beloved adopted home.

What if my parents hadn't left Serbia? What if I hadn't grown up in a refugee camp? What if I weren't an American?

In my childhood, although we were still quite poor by American standards, every three months my mother sent each of her five sisters in Yugoslavia a much-needed care package of powdered eggs and milk and dented-can food. What if?

The first time I visited Yugoslavia, while traveling as a college student, I learned that six of my cousins had shared one large bed in the only room other than a tiny kitchen—a bed I was sharing with the youngest ones who still lived at home. What if?

And here in Habana, what if these dark spaces I was now entering had sheltered me instead of these Cuban people?

This is the litany that plays in my mind. This is the fear that won't let go, the dark place I need to explore.

So I wander the streets and enter the shadowy spaces in which mysteries grow more familiar by the day, looking to merge my present with my past.

When my young cousin comes from Serbia and wishes he could figure out—in these days of intense immigration repression—some way to stay in America, I wonder: Why me?

When I learn another cousin in Belgrade sleeps downstairs in the winter because she cannot afford to fix the leak in her roof, I wonder: Why me?

When I walk into dark ruins in Havana and meet a broadly grinning woman who offers coffee in her closet-sized hovel, I wonder: Why me?

And so, shifting between the torment of *what if?* and *why me?* I reach out to those I meet. I give them my smile, my caring words, my respect. But for their strength and their brave acceptance of reality, I would give them my tears.

After a few days, I went back to see Estrella and bring her a trinket from San Francisco. This time I strode confidently into the arched doorway. After all, I was entering a friend's home. I eyed the floral metal art deco bannisters on the stairway, the fading grandeur of warm-toned plaster of Paris. I stepped over broken beams and past chips of stucco.

I met Estrella's daughter, who lived next door, along a perilous walkway. I told her how her mother had saved my life from the ferocious dog. We laughed together as neighbors passed on their way out.

My mind went to a visit with my aunt in Belgrade in 1968. We stood at her back door and neighbors wandered down the open wooden staircase, greeting her and stopping to chat. It felt warm and friendly, and I told her how much my father missed that camaraderie. "Yes . . . but . . ." she said, "he might not miss it so much if he couldn't escape it, as I can't." Her reply helped me see that it was a lack of alternatives, poverty and crowding that facilitated this lifestyle my father romanticized.

And so I am torn between a father forced to flee who never quite recovered and a mother who joined her husband in exile but adapted to make America her home. I am torn by my sorrow and anguish over his shattered life, his regret of what might have been. By my grief that I never knew the successful young man who captured my mother's heart.

The shattered Habana Vieja I explore brings me closer to the truth in my own life, and I start understanding what I am seeking. Somewhere in those dark spaces I might even find myself.

What if?

Why me?

Why *not* me?

Image from the documentary *Maestra*, about the Cuban Literacy Campaign of 1961

Another Kind of Hero
Donna Hemmila

When I asked Cubans what was the most important thing to see in Havana, they all directed me to the Museo de la Revolución. Housed in the pre-revolutionary Presidential Palace, its rambling collection tells the story of battles fought, hardships endured, and social changes hard-won. The artifacts on display keep the revolutionary legends alive: Che's iconic beret, Fidel's and his brother Raul's shiny black combat boots, rifles, short-wave radios, uniforms—the ephemera of revolutionary lives lived and sacrificed, dispensed with an overdose of *machismo*.

As I navigated through the museum, I also discovered the history of less flashy, yet equally relevant, Revolutionary heroes, *los maestros*, the teachers. Behind a glass display case, photos and text told the story of the Cuban Literacy Campaign, a chapter in the Revolution as dramatic and heroic to me as the battles fought in the Sierra Maestra mountain range.

In 1961, the Revolutionary government launched a year-long campaign to teach its poor, rural citizens to read and write. Armed with books, pencils, paper, and kerosene lanterns, more than 250,000 young volunteers—half of them women, half of them teenagers—left home to live and teach in the mountains and countryside. Since there was no electricity, the lanterns became not only a symbol of the shining light of knowledge but also an indispensable tool. Most of the teaching had to take place at night after the students finished working in the fields.

As I gazed at the museum photos of these brave volunteers, I imagined myself one of them, walking through the countryside wearing a beret, carrying my lantern overhead, or marching in a celebratory parade waving a five-foot-long pencil. I was fourteen at the time, but so were many of the volunteers who joined the campaign. If I had been born in Cuba, for sure, teaching would have been my Revolutionary calling. However, it's more likely I'd have been one of the students.

I experienced my own period of illiteracy when I entered first grade. I still remember the humiliation of standing at the front of the classroom, holding a wooden pointer hovering over the yellow construction paper capital "G" tacked above the blackboard. Not only did I not know how to read, I didn't even know the whole alphabet. There I stood in front of my classmates, stalled at "G," feeling frightened and very small. I was ignorant, and, until then, didn't even know it. After this public shaming, the nun assigned me to the "D" reading group, the lowest of the low.

It's not that my parents were illiterate. They were young and poor. It never occurred to them that they should teach me to read. Once the floodgates of knowledge opened, however, I quickly worked my way up to the "A" reading group. I was bookish after all.

But that did not mean I had books of my own. I had comic books and Little Golden Books, those children's picture books sold in grocery and dime stores for twenty-five cents. Once I learned to read, our mother would walk my sister and me to the public library where we could borrow stacks of books. But it wasn't the same as having forever books, ones I never had to give back.

When I reached my early twenties, the years of yearning for books ended. Finally, I could afford to buy them. My personal library expanded along with my earning power. I grew into one of those book-obsessed people, a true *abibliophobiac,* one who suffers from an irrational fear of running out of reading material. Books fill every nook in my home, stacks and stacks of books. To me, a life without books is a tragedy.

This obsessive book-love is what drew me to Cuba Libro, where another literacy campaign is underway.

Founded by American ex-pat journalist Conner Gorry, Cuba Libro is the first and only English-language bookstore on the entire island. Since donated books make up the store's inventory, before I left for Cuba, I asked Conner what titles they needed. The eclectic list she sent contained classics from Hemingway and Fitzgerald, current literature, travel books, and music and home improvement magazines. I set to work collecting books, hitting up my traveling companions for donations.

After our group arrived in Havana, five of us set aside an afternoon to visit Cuba Libro and deliver our bags of books. When we arrived in the Havana neighborhood of Vedado, where the bookstore is located, we found so much more than a purveyor of books.

The sign out front reads "café, bookstore, oasis." In addition to selling books, Cuba Libro functions as a community resource for its neighbors. Conner and her small staff hold garage sales, give away condoms and other health-care supplies, donate books to primary schools, and raise money to find homes for the city's stray dogs and cats. It's an art gallery, coffee shop, and home for writing workshops.

Cuba Libro is all of those thing, plus a vibrant community resource for learning English, the global language of business and technology. The urgency to acquire English skills is growing. In the same way learning to read and write opened opportunities for Cubans after the Revolution, today learning to read, write and speak English increases job prospects for Cubans at home and abroad. In fact, a recent policy change requires university students to pass an English competency exam to earn a degree.

"We get a lot of first-year university students asking for book recommendations," Conner told us as we sipped cappuccinos in an art- and book-filled corner of Cuba Libro. "One of their first assignments is to write a book report."

Cuba Libro operates as a co-operative with profit sharing. Along with job training, Conner provides the staff with English classes.

The priciest book in the store costs the equivalent of five U.S. dollars. For five pesos, anyone can rent a book for two weeks.

"We're getting rid of financial barriers to access books," Conner said. "Some of our happiest moments are when we can pair up people with a book. *V for Vendetta* came in yesterday, and we had three people fighting over it."

But patrons don't need to spend money to access reading material. Cuba Libro doesn't mind customers reading for free. When we visited, a cluster of young Cubans, engrossed in books and magazines, occupied the hammocks that hang in the shady front patio. Prior to the Revolution, only the privileged few would have had the leisure time or ability to spend an afternoon reading in a hammock. The brave *maestros* of the Literary Campaign shined a light that can never be dimmed.

Miriam, a friend of one of our Cuban guides, was eighteen when she volunteered to teach in Baracoa. She had graduated as a teacher and was put in charge of ten other young teachers, five boys and five girls. More than 700,000 adults learned to read and write during the year the campaign flourished. Today, Cuba boasts a literacy rate of 99.75 percent, according to UNESCO statistics, well above the global rate of 86.24 percent.

"The best thing about the experience was our happiness for being involved in something like that," Miriam remembers. "After a few days, we felt we were part of those families. When it was time for us to leave, we even cried."

When the campaign ended, Miriam returned to Camagüey to teach.

"After the Revolution, the police barracks became scholar cities, so that meant a lot," she says. "It was a privilege for me. The job we did was very well acknowledged, and we appreciated it."

I can't help thinking the job *los maestros* did hasn't been acknowledged enough. Havana once housed a museum honoring the campaign. After three attempts to locate it, on my last afternoon in Havana I encountered a young woman who showed me where it had been and informed me it had moved. The Cuban Literacy Campaign Museum now lies about nine miles southwest of central Havana in Marianao, a municipality not many foreign visitors are likely to seek out. On my next trip to Cuba, I intend to pay my respects to this little museum. But I need to see the story of *los maestros* bursting out of museum display cases.

I couldn't go anywhere in Cuba without running into the faces of the Revolution. Billboards honoring Fidel Castro dot highways. A giant image of Che Guevara stares out from the side of a seven-story government building. Postcards, T-shirts and murals immortalize the country's heroes. Certainly the heroes of the Literacy Campaign deserve equal treatment. Murals? Billboards? Perhaps a monument in the center of Habana Viejo? Maybe someday I'll even be able to buy a T-shirt emblazoned with the proud, smiling face of a *maestro*.

Photo in the Museo de Playa Girón near Cienfuego

¿Viva la Revolución?

Douglas Hale

I could never get angry with Fidel, Fidel Castro Ruz. Despite the murders, imprisonments, property seizures and the loss of liberty, the memories from my eight-year-old self haunted me all my life. Anyone able to make the horror of Fulgencio Batista's regime that I saw go away could be forgiven most anything.

Sixty-three years later I returned to Cuba in late 2017, hoping to find the nightmare that I briefly witnessed in pre-revolutionary Cuba ended, and eager to learn what had replaced it.

I came to be in Cuba in September 1955 because my father's three-year tour of duty at an airbase in Puerto Rico had ended, and we were returning home. On our way to New York City our ship stopped in Guantanamo, Cuba, for a few days. That is when our parents decided my brothers and I needed to see the Cuban countryside. So we boarded a military bus and headed into the mountains—seventy miles to the east of the mountains that would within fifteen months harbor Fidel, Che Guevara and their soldiers.

The settlements we passed were familiar from our first years in Puerto Rico—just clusters of shacks spread around the perimeter of a clearing. But there were none of the concrete-block bungalows that had sprung up throughout Puerto Rico. What really got our attention were kids about our ages.

By contrast to Puerto Rican kids, almost all of the Cuban children were half or completely naked. They weren't running or playing, but just sitting or standing around. Even though all of them were skinny, many looked to us like they had swallowed a soccer ball. Neither my brother Greg nor I knew what we were seeing, but we knew it was bad.

When the jungle and sugar cane fields gave way to pastures, we would amuse ourselves by counting the ribs of cattle. Fifty, seventy-five yards away made no difference: We could clearly see their ribs. And unlike in Puerto Rico, the chickens pecking in the dirt were the size of softballs. We had never seen such tiny chickens.

We also knew that compared to Cuba, Puerto Rico was paradise. How could it be that Puerto Ricans who had been so poor in 1951, much like the Cubans we had seen from the bus, were now relatively wealthy, while the Cubans remained in abject poverty? The questions haunted me throughout my youth and led me in adulthood to become an economist—an embryonic science to improve the material lives of people. Six decades and many American travel bans and sanctions later, I came to Cuba with my traveling companion Gloriann to see how the descendants of the people I had witnessed so long ago lived now.

Our investigation was to start at Santiago de Cuba, but first we had to get there. We landed at Holguin and squeezed into a private car, which fortuitously took us by Birán, Fidel's birthplace and boyhood home. Fidel's illiterate father Ángel Castro y Argiz came from Spain in 1905 and over the following twenty years became wealthy from hard physical work, and from selling to travelers on the main Havana-Santiago de Cuba road that crossed his land. Don

Ángel built a school and invited all the local children to come there for free. When he had trouble hiring teachers, he built the teacher's house next to the school. Fidel, born in 1926, attended that school—but with his sharp mind and photographic memory he soon outgrew it. Eventually he attended the Jesuit Belén High School in Havana where he excelled. His grounding in Catholic teachings later helped in his extensive meetings with three popes. In Birán, I felt I'd seen the origins of Fidel's commitment to education, health and reasoned argument.

But had Fidel and Che's Revolution, Soviet aid, and a communist economy delivered on their promise of a better life? To find answers, again I took a rural bus ride, this time from Santiago on Cuba's southeast coast through the city of Guantanamo, then to Baracoa near Cuba's northeast corner.

During the five-hour bus ride, Gloriann and I passed many homes and small towns that are strung along the road to Baracoa. From the bus's window, wooden shacks, often far removed from the road, were clearly visible. But for each shack, this time there were dozens of modest bungalows, most with patios and flower gardens. Some appeared to have vegetable gardens "out back" along with chickens and a few horses.

The cows, horses, chickens, goats and occasional pig we saw in the country appeared well-fed and healthy looking. So were the horses and chickens within Baracoa and the cows and pigs visible on the outskirts of town. Eventually, on a rutted road leading to a cocoa plantation, we came upon two skinny horses tied to a bush. I could have counted their ribs. They were the only undernourished or unhealthy farm animals I saw in Cuba.

In the small towns we found one- and two-story concrete buildings in various states of repair shoved together to form a "poor man's" strip mall stretching a city block. Grim, unappealing but not Soviet ugly. Each town boasted a colorfully painted school and medical center sitting in a landscaped mini-park. There were no signs of trash, peeling paint, broken windows or doors. The schools had baseball or soccer fields or a playground with equipment such as a jungle gym.

Much to my relief the children seemed normal—healthy, animated, running around kicking soccer balls and huddling with groups of their friends before school. Surprisingly, I did not hear a lot of laughter; Cuban kids, though friendly, have a serious air about them. I did not see any street confrontations, but often saw kids walking around alone or in pairs at night—none sporting "gangsta" wear. In fact, Cuba's fashion stars are the kids. Everywhere their uniforms were well tailored and attractive; even the boys kept their white shirts clean.

Furthermore, people across Cuba appeared to be fed and clothed. No one I saw was reduced to wearing rags. Begging and obesity are rare. Perhaps this is because, having no other choice, Cubans walk everywhere, carrying groceries, furniture and TVs. Having no lifts, they climb endless stairs.

The Cuban people I met represent the best of Fidel's legacy: an educated, well-fed, healthy populace. My impressions are borne out by statistics. According to Cuba's 1953 Census one quarter of the population was illiterate. By 1970 nearly all Cubans were literate. Cuba has continued to invest 12.8 percent of its GDP in education—among the highest percentages in the world, whereas, according to the CIA Fact Book, the United States invests 4.9 percent.

Similarly, Cuban life expectancy at the start of the Castro regime was 63.9 years compared to Puerto Rico's 68.7 years and the United States' 69.7. By 2015 Cuba and Puerto Rico enjoyed the same life expectancy: 79.5 years, about a year longer than continental Americans.

But statistics don't reveal the surprise and delight I constantly found meeting everyday people. One night in central Cienfuegos, Gloriann and I reluctantly took a pedicab the two miles back to our *casa particular*. Our driver/peddler—a plump, late thirty-something elf—gabbed on and on. We both complimented him on his English, but I noted a slight New York City accent. "Did you learn English in school? Did you spend time in New York City?" I asked.

He replied: "No I got my MBA in school. I learned English watching *Seinfeld*. I started by making the sounds without knowing their meaning. I didn't like George's voice so I mimicked Jerry. I am working on French now, but there are fewer pirated French DVDs out there ... not like the American stuff. We have all your TV shows and movies." We tipped him double his fare.

From what I could see across Cuba, the Revolution had exorcised the horrors I witnessed as a child. That is no small accomplishment. But that is also not the end of the story. Everywhere I heard the rumblings: "A revolution is coming, and it is coming soon." Facts and observations verify the need for change. Cuba imports about 80 percent of its food but about 40 percent of its cultivable land lies fallow.

Whenever I walked outside well-preserved central plazas in Santiago, Baracoa, Havana or Matanzas, I saw formerly magnificent hundred-year-old stone and brick buildings crumbling, some collapsed upon themselves or in advanced decay. Baracoa, for example, struggling to rebuild following Hurricane Matthew a year earlier, broke my heart. Almost every block had rows of battered one- to three-story buildings, some without roofs, others covered by a makeshift patchwork of tarps, tin sheets and random boards.

In several cities, buildings closer to the sea fare worse. Entire blocks are reduced to empty lots. The skin of five- and six-story apartment buildings is stripped off, revealing naked concrete, roofs blown off and few windows intact. Many have been "red tagged" but people still live in them. They have no place else to go.

Everyday consumer goods are in short supply throughout the island: flashlights, soap, ballpoint pens, paper and books. People, including staff at the *casas particulares*, were thrilled when I left such items behind.

The roads are full of sixty-year-old mostly American cars still running and spewing smoke. Even the Russian death traps I rode in are prized. But with dilapidation comes patience. Alongside major roads and intersections, people congregate waiting for hours hoping to catch a ride. Lines of people wait outside government stores that have something to sell. People sit for hours in central plazas or outside tourist hotels hoping to secure an Internet connection.

Wages are abysmal. The second evening of our trip, Gloriann and I and a friend paid about seventy dollars for three dinners, drinks and wine. That's when we learned that we had spent the equivalent of a month's pay for a doctor, while our modest lunches were equal to a month's pay of Cuba's highest-earning nurses.

Wages remain low despite the highly educated and ambitious workforce. At the La Terraza-Casa Nilson Paladar in Baracoa, I complimented our waiter on his excellent English. We began discussing education in Cuba, and I was shocked by revelations I heard repeatedly: "See him, the bar keeper? He is a chemical engineer; the maître d' is a physicist; the busboy is a computer scientist; me, I am a mechanical engineer. We work here because there are no jobs and the few there are pay nothing. Fidel educated us, but he forgot someone has to work the fields."

In particular, the tension between their great potential and their limited prospects frustrates all the young people we met. The images they see on pirated TV shows just add to the pain. Partially in response to those pressures, Raúl Castro opened the economy in 2011 to some private enterprise in a few areas including *casas particulares, paladars* and organic foods. Already they provide the best meals and service in Cuba.

The economic opening has spawned a renaissance of reconstruction. In Santiago de Cuba, for example, alongside collapsed and collapsing buildings, newly renovated buildings housing *casa particulares, paladars,* organic markets, apartments, galleries and other commercial activities are springing up. On most blocks, construction materials—bags of sand, piles of rebar, mounds of stone, bundles of tiles—spill onto the sidewalk in full view and remain unguarded, waiting for the next reconstruction project.

Even in the disaster zone that is Baracoa, people are rebuilding and refurbishing homes and businesses. My own *casa particular* had a beautiful tile floor, a comfortable bed, a fully modern bathroom and a refrigerator (without enough beer). A few blocks away, shoulder to shoulder with a bunker-like metalworking and repair shop, I saw another elegant home under construction featuring a three-car garage, exquisite tile work and patio banisters ending in polo pony heads.

Despite these efforts, the pressures for change are building. Hence the talk of revolution. No one I met advocated a violent housecleaning. Most wanted the government to keep doing what it does well—provide education, medical care, national guard/ emergency services—and to step out of the way of innovation. No one saw American-style income inequality as desirable. No one had anything good to say about a Soviet-style economy.

The waste of resources—human energy and talent, arable land, the nation's capital stock and its natural endowment—and the human suffering it brings, are an economist's nightmare. My hope is that the fruit of Fidel's Revolution—a healthy and educated populace—will seed an evolution ending this nightmare.

Filmmaker Miguel Coyula

BEING NADIE
Linda Jue

Miguel Coyula does not exist. He can't seek employment because he doesn't exist. He can't run a thriving business because he can't hire anybody or sell any goods or services. Nor can he attend many social or public functions. People generally don't acknowledge him, much less associate with him, because he simply does not exist.

Miguel Coyula is *nadie*. Nobody. The Cuban government has rendered him a ghost in his own country. His crime? Committing unbridled artistic expression.

An internationally recognized independent filmmaker, Miguel is as well known for his stubborn streak as he is for his films. He brooks no interference in any aspect of his productions, least of all dictates on content. Unlike other filmmakers, Miguel even refuses to delegate common operational tasks to a film crew. He insists on doing his own scriptwriting, directing, cinematography, editing, sound design … you name it. He does it all, and all by himself. It's no wonder his artistic intransigence infuriates a lot of people. Not just the government, but the entire community of Cuban filmmakers.

I first encountered Miguel's work through a mutual friend who suggested I meet Miguel during my trip to Cuba. As an introduction, our friend played Miguel's widely acclaimed documentary profiling another nobody, appropriately titled, *Nadie*.

In the film, Rafael Alcides, celebrated poet and writer of the Cuban Revolution, laments the loss of dozens of his unpublished works as the homemade typewriter ink fades off their pages. Almost all his philosophical and political ideas are literally disappearing before his eyes, and he can feel himself melting away with them. Half blind and half deaf, and somewhere in his eighties, Alcides knows he can only salvage a fraction of the manuscripts.

At one time, this now banished poet and influential thinker was such a passionate champion of the Revolution that he would extol its wonders as if—by his own admission—it were a woman and he, her lover. Remnants of that fervor still come across on-screen as he reflects back on the early days of the new regime.

"What a beautiful thing, this Revolution," he says, as a wave of emotion sweeps across his face. He can barely get his words out without pausing to maintain his composure.

"It was … such a moment … a beautiful thing …. There are no words to talk about this … no words …. Those are the things one would like to bring back …. But they fucked all this up. They blew it."

Fidel's growing authoritarian rule and the increasing corruption within the regime broke the spell for Alcides. The final disillusionment came when the Soviets invaded Czechoslovakia in 1968. Alcides objected to what he saw as Fidel's hypocrisy for speaking out against U.S. invasions of other countries while not protesting the Soviet crackdown on the Czechs, who were calling for liberal reforms. He walked away from the Revolution in disgust, like a betrayed lover, disappearing from public life from that moment on. By his own choice, he became *nadie*.

As I watch Miguel Coyula's film about Alcides, the unusual film techniques immediately capture my attention. To break up the monotony of Alcides's talking head against a black background, Miguel digitally inserts and manipulates a running collage of images and sounds taken from a variety of sources, such as old movies, photographs, periodicals, TV and radio broadcasts, and music recordings. He employs some of the images to create the illusion that Alcides is actually talking with Fidel. He also uses an actress, who I later learn is his wife, to embody the soul of the Revolution as a woman—with whom Alcides appears to interact. The serial collage evokes visual and auditory impressions of Alcides's words that seem to speak to me at some deeper level than mere listening can reach. They impart a barely palpable yet nagging surreal quality to my experience of the film, leaving me feeling intangibly haunted by the end.

Miguel Coyula is indeed no ordinary filmmaker. He's an exceptionally creative visual artist for whom film is his medium rather than the canvas, and who has had to innovate without money, crew or technical resources. It's obvious why he's won accolades outside Cuba, from a Guggenheim Fellowship to many awards at film festivals around the world.

It's also clear why the Cuban government wants Miguel to pay the price for his insistent (some would say petulant) individualism. It has tried to intimidate him, even manufacturing situations that would justify carting him off to jail—though they have yet to succeed in either. So far, he gets to remain in his nice Havana apartment with his wife. He has his ration card like everyone else. He can even travel outside the country to earn money. But the government has made sure that Miguel can never be recognized or earn a living in Cuba again.

Several weeks after viewing the film, I'm sitting across from this ghost in his well-appointed apartment in Havana's Vedado district.

Elegant chinoiserie furniture and *objets* fill the living and dining rooms. Although he had inherited the apartment and its furnishings from relatives, the fact Miguel lives there has fueled resentment among other filmmakers who also falsely assume he is making lots of money abroad.

Given his reputation as the bad boy of Cuban cinema, I was expecting a formidable-looking figure with a Type Triple A personality. Instead, the youngish forty-year-old man before me is gracious and unassuming. Dressed in T-shirt, shorts and flip-flops, his dark hair pulled back in a ponytail, with a beard accenting a gentle-looking countenance, he's the picture of mellowness.

Miguel briefly demonstrates how he manipulated images to create his desired effects in *Nadie*. In one example, he combined three paintings by a famous Cuban artist to produce an entirely new, realistic-looking work of art.

"The idea for this documentary is that nothing is in a pure state," says Miguel. "In the interview with Alcides, images are always being altered in front of and behind him."

I realize that almost every idea Alcides expresses in the film is inflected with Miguel's own interpretations through his imagery and sounds. We're not only watching and hearing Alcides's thoughts but Miguel's as well. At times, the images feel like a moving painting. At others, they're like hyperkinetic cartoons gone in a flash. They reflect as much Miguel's disillusionment with the Revolution as they do Alcides's. *Nadie* isn't just a documentary; it's an art form. And apparently, all his films share this same cinematic language.

"Your films require a visual literacy that a lot of people don't have," I remark.

"Yeah," he replies. "You have to have a dialogue with the images. Otherwise, it's impossible." He acknowledges that his films have been inaccessible for even some art house audiences. His current film, which he's secretly making, is even more extreme, he says. It's a sci-fi takedown of Fidel's concept of the ideal socialist man.

Miguel explains that he teaches for a month at different American universities every year, including the Ivy Leagues. His earnings cover his living and production expenses. But he has nothing left for luxuries like computer repairs. His penurious life partially explains why he does his own production work.

Going back to *Nadie*, I ask how he found Alcides and got him to agree to be filmed.

"He lives not far from here, actually .... He's married to my cousin. Since I was a little boy I go to his home."

But it wasn't a simple matter of family privilege. Alcides saw the camera as the only way to preserve his writings. Everything he talks about is essentially a recapitulation of ideas from his manuscripts. Those ideas spoke poignantly to Miguel's own disaffection with the Revolution and the current state of his country.

Miguel grew up during the 1980s, at the height of the economic bonanza subsidized by the Soviets, which offset the impact of the U.S. embargo on Cuba. Those subsidies evaporated with the 1991 collapse of the U.S.S.R., initiating the "Special Period," the Cuban government's euphemism for the catastrophic devastation of the country's economy. That crisis shredded Miguel's socialist idealism.

"I became critical not only of Cuban society, but of any society in the world because, in the back of your head, you're still looking for those ideals of social justice. You can't walk away from that. When we were kids we were told that by the year 2000 there wouldn't be any money, because it was the utopia of communism. So there's a part of us that's dysfunctional in any society we're faced with because of that."

At that moment, Miguel's wife, Lynn, arrives. An accomplished playwright as well as an actress, she's as congenial and passionate as he is. Together, they paint a far less romanticized picture of Cuba than the one many foreigners harbor.

"We know that a lot of people outside of Cuba need to believe that the Revolution is still a dream," says Lynn. "The truth is, Cubans everywhere are unhappy. We're all trying to find another way to live. We don't have social justice anymore."

"The biggest accomplishments of the Revolution," says Miguel, "which were free health care and education, are highly corrupt. Parents have to bribe teachers to guarantee their kids get good grades. The teachers demand presents of no less than five CUCs. Also, when you go to the doctor, you need money to bribe the doctor to get medicine because that doctor has a limited amount, and of course, he will give the medicine to whoever bribes him the most. It's almost institutionalized corruption."

Miguel and Lynn say the government began to exert more control over all artists since Barack Obama restored relations because it doesn't want Americans exposed to Cuba's domestic critics. But cell phones, computers and the Internet thwart those efforts, allowing a growing number of younger artists to produce works that defy the censors. Hence, security forces have become more draconian in their dealings with artists.

"Are you afraid of going to jail?" I ask Miguel.

"I'm ready for it … if I have to go to jail or die," he replies emphatically. "Because there are so few things we can control in life, and I found that making films the way I want to is the one thing that makes me sleep well at night. If I can't have that …"

The government actually did blockade the opening of Lynn's play, directed by Miguel, the previous week. Both would have been detained except for the dozens of cell phones recording the incident. The government has also begun to deny requests by international film festivals to screen Cuban films if Miguel's works are included, setting up a powerful obstacle to his films being entered at these events. However, the chances of Miguel ever facing prison are slim.

"The ones that really worry the government are artists with political ambitions," he says. "I don't have any."

Miguel says that almost all of Cuba's best filmmakers have left the country because of the straitened economy and heightened censorship. He's staying because he doesn't have to worry about housing or basic living expenses, which allows him to work on his films, albeit as *nadie*. Like Alcides, Miguel believes the artist's responsibility is to hold a mirror up to society and reveal its contradictions, and he intends to keep doing so no matter what.

Our conversation has certainly answered why I've had similar feelings about Cuba since landing on the island as I did watching Miguel's film. The country is a feast of contradictions.

Still, music fills the air everywhere, from early morning till late evening. Residents actually open their doors and windows to let the familiar Cuban rhythms blare out into the streets. The *joie de vivre* so evident among the people seems to propel them forward with ingenuity and pluck, Miguel being a prime example. His adamant protectiveness of his creative process, while extreme to many, gives me courage to face my own creative demons. And the privilege of becoming acquainted with the thinking of two of Cuba's most eloquent *nadies* gives me hope for rescuing my own teetering idealism as an American in these troubled times.

This billboard between Havana and the airport characterizes the American-initiated blockade as genocide.

CUBA: IT'S COMPLICATED
MJ Pramik

A postcard on my refrigerator:
"*Un mundo mejor es possible ...*" Fidel Castro.
I read it every day. Surreal. The "communist" dictator said this. Cuba: It is so complicated.

The rhythm of "Chan Chan" rocked my dreams as the air-conditioned bus turned and surged through the poorer neighborhoods of Havana while we toured the city on my first visit to the island in 2015, before the opening of the U.S.-Cuba detente. The luxury of my aseptic, odorless ride juxtaposed against the tropical environs of the people strolling through Havana's sweltering heat.

"Cuba: It's complicated," Zoe said with a wry smile, microphone covering her brightly-hued lips. This mantra often prefaced any intriguing new fact dispensed by our young tour guide during my first foray onto this Caribbean island a few months before President Barack Obama opened up talks between the two countries. I'd fallen in love with Cuba when Wim Wenders's *Buena Vista Social Club* premiered in San Francisco nearly twenty years ago. And long before I saw the film, I harbored a fascination with the tiny island that stood up and resisted the giant United States in the name of stamping out corruption and working for "the people." Of course, as a child, I always played Tonto to my playmates' Lone Ranger.

Magical realism: a genre in which realistic tales and naturalistic ritual intermingle with surreal elements of dream fantasy. To my way of thinking, Cubans celebrate such a life—a life of magical realism.

Zoe recounted how, after the overthrow of U.S.-backed dictator Fulgencio Batista, the moneyed elite were given an option: stay and share their wealth with all Cubans, or leave. The (mostly white) upper classes fled to Miami and other points north. The Castro Revolutionary government confiscated properties and money, threw out the mafia, and established a socialist government with free schools for all children and a free university education if one so chose, as well as universal medical care. They also published government propaganda, executed and imprisoned Revolution resisters, and caused severe food and toilet paper shortages, among a multitude of unpleasant issues.

"Back in the days," the 26-year-old Zoe, who is of light-skinned Spanish ancestry, would start each story of the Revolution versus the Batista dictatorship and U.S. imperialism. *The days* were in the 1950s, when a little girl like myself grew up in Ike's imperialist America. Listening to Zoe speak, I admired the spirit and intent of the 26th of July Movement. Politics aside, having all Cubans share in the country's wealth—and poverty—remains a noble adventure. Free health care for all, food shared equally with each Cuban issued a monthly ration card, a high literacy rate (99.76% in 2012, second only to Azerbaijan), education based on aptitude, and a visible caring for each other—I witnessed these basic effects of Castro's regime wherever Zoe led us. I also witnessed intense poverty. I saw men tilling in the fields with a mule pulling a metal plow. How much of this scarcity and privation can be blamed on the Castro dictatorship or the U.S. embargo that twisted the arms of countries worldwide to not trade with Cuba is still debated.

However, I saw very few homeless resembling the street people of our major U.S. cities.

According to Zoe, if an uncle or cousin is found sleeping on a park bench in Cuba, a family member is bound to bring them home.

The portraits we in America see of Cuba often contradict each other. American news outlets continue to post stories of torture and repression of the people. The recent "sonic attack" of U.S. diplomats that caused the American government to expel fifteen Cuban diplomats may not have actually occurred. Fake news abounds. Reese Erlich, syndicated columnist on international affairs, noted that the current administration would not allow press interviews with any of the U.S. "victims."

American and Cuban films depict the Castro regime's horrific persecution of gays and unmistakable underlying racism toward those of African descent. Many white Americans associate Castro with communism and dictatorship, however, many African Americans associate Fidel with liberation because he met with Malcolm X and granted former Black Liberation Army's Assata Shakur political asylum. Castro's anticolonial skirmishes in Latin America have led some scholars to weigh his honorable struggle for the common good against his racial prejudices and his extinguishing of dissent by imprisoning anyone who might have a dissenting thought. Some in Cuba still feel the sting of being watched daily.

Cuba. It's complicated.

Due to the unwarranted ongoing U.S. embargo against Cuba after the failed 1961 Bay of Pigs invasion, Castro turned to Russia to help his people. After a period of prosperity through trade, the Russians left when the Soviet Union dissolved in 1991, and the "Special

Period" of the 1990s caused severe economic hardships in Cuba. Food often grew scarce, even with government ration cards. But the Cuban people survived. They did not revolt against and overturn the Castro government, as their northern neighbor country had hoped. Magical realism indeed. An uprising of sorts occurred in August, 1994, against the deprivations of the Special Period that saw thousands take to the streets of Havana chanting *"Libertad!"* But Cuban security forces dispersed the demonstrators after only a few hours. The protests waned as quickly as an uproarious sea wind.

"I'd never leave Cuba," Zoe reflected. "This country's given me a great free education and my parents have free medical care. I want to travel, to see the world, but I would always come back. My family is here."

An enormous shrine to Cuba's magical realism is *Escuela Latinoamericana de Medicina* or ELAM. In 2015, I toured the Latin American School of Medicine started by Fidel Castro and the Revolutionary government in 1999. Located at the old Naval Academy west of Havana on a stunning beach overlooking deep blue waters, this medical school, with the largest enrollment in the world, is operated by the Cuban government. Over 19,550 students from across the globe study in the eighty classrooms, thirty-seven laboratories, five amphitheaters, one huge infirmary, and countless dormitories, to become medical doctors. They return to their home countries—Ghana, Pakistan, all parts of Africa, and the United States—with solid medical training.

That's where I met Nikolai "Nick" Casanova, one of over one hundred Americans working toward their doctor of medicine degree … *for free*. In the United States, getting an MD usually saddles a graduate with three hundred thousand dollars of debt, often influencing which medical specialty the newly minted physician chooses. A brain surgeon can dispense with the student debt much faster than a low earning general practitioner or pediatrician.

"I love Cuban medicine!" Nick grinned during our second meeting a few months ago in Havana. He'd taken a few hours out of his busy OB/GYN rotation to meet me in Old Havana. His enthusiasm for caring for people bubbled over. In his presence, I felt a deep faith in the goodness of humanity.

Each ELAM student receives a scholarship of full tuition with housing. Also included are three meals a day, medical textbooks, Spanish courses, uniforms, toiletries, bedding, and a stipend of one hundred Cuban pesos (four U.S. dollars) per month. In return, they perform a one-year rotating internship at one of Cuba's training hospitals.

"I googled free medical school one day and ELAM popped up." Nick described his first step in the journey to Cuba. An X-ray technician in New York with a biology degree, Nick knew his single mother could not afford to pay the hefty medical school costs in the United States. So he applied to ELAM, found sponsorship through a church group, entered Cuba via Mexico, and started his training. Nick, born in Jamaica and now a U.S. citizen living in the Bronx, will graduate in 2020 after seven or so years and enter medicine as a general practitioner. An emergency medicine physician in New York named Dr. Michael I. Griffin oversees the transition program for American students, who must pass three medical board exams to qualify for the MD degree. The ELAM curriculum is fully accredited by the Medical Board of California and recognized by the World Health Organization as well as the Educational Commission for Foreign Medical Graduates.

"I want to serve rural communities in the U.S. where there's a lack of doctors." Nick beamed a broad smile when he met me for a quick drink in Old Havana. Nick can go into general practice because he will not have hundreds of thousands of dollars of debt to repay. I felt Nick's enthusiasm about his future. His excitement about Cuban medicine set me thinking about checking out ELAM. (I did. I'm too old to start the program.)

"In Cuba, physicians make house calls and treat the entire family. We talk to everyone when we examine an elderly patient or an infant. We spend time with them. It's not the HMO model of the fifteen-minute push." He related how the Cuban government performed a countrywide education about the Zika virus, with tutorials for the entire population and healthcare workers doing outreach. Back in the United States, I've often reflected (as a science writer) on how we read about the Zika invasion through alarming news stories.

"The Cuban people are a happy people. They are very family oriented," Nick emphasized. From the American press, we learned of so many boats of people fleeing the island. Particularly heartrending was the story of Elián González, whose mother drowned crossing to Miami with her young son. Elián returned to Cuba to live with his father and half-brothers, and now works as an engineer. Not all Cubans stand ready to swim to the northern country that has them in a stranglehold of sanctions. Nick's testimonials to the spirit of the Cuban people told me otherwise. Was Nick caught up in the magic of this Caribbean island too?

"But hey! We just have to come together and make this country and world a better place. We're all going to make money somehow. We really don't have to make more than we need," said Nick, always smiling. We parted on Calle Obispo, with me so wishing I lived in whichever rural American town where Nick would practice in about three years. His spirit soared beyond the Hippocratic Oath, beyond "do no harm" to "do good." Now *that's* magical realism in today's world of narcissism and greed.

As I began to pack my things to head home, I paused to reflect on my favorite revelation from my research: Fidel Castro served as the unofficial copy editor to Gabriel García Márquez. They forged a deep friendship after meeting in a Cuban hotel in 1977, according to Stéphanie Panichelli-Batella and Angel Estaban in their 2009 book *Fidel & Gabo*. After he found mistakes in the calculation of boat speed in Gabriel García Márquez's *The Story of a Shipwrecked Sailor*, Castro offered to read the Columbian Nobel laureate's texts for fact checking. Gabriel García Márquez sent each manuscript to Fidel, who affectionately called him "Gabo." A note written to him by Castro in 2010 during Cuba's response to the Haiti earthquake has Fidel noting the devastation "reminded me of *Love in the Time of Cholera*." Gabo mentioned in an interview that he would criticize the Cuban dictator to his face, but only in private. Never before the world.

I consider this relationship quite amazing. I read *One Hundred Years of Solitude* twice in my twenties, savoring each delicious scene and dreamlike sketch as I approached full-fledged adulthood. As a white (Polish now qualifies as "white"… back in the days when I grew up in rural Ohio, not so much), liberal, progressive writer, I tend to have an open limbic system. The dualism of magical realism has always intrinsically made sense to me.

At the end of my second visit to Cuba in 2017, I walked the streets of Havana, old and new, feeling safe and peaceful. Trekking to the Malecón each morning past fishermen or strolling the seawall at night among lovers (it's nicknamed "the living room"), complicated seems good. I admire the intricate, often problematic nature of this experiment of a country. Another surreal, mysterious aspect of Cuba: no street bears Castro's name. Not one statue hovers over any square. The legacy he aimed for is witnessed in the people. T-shirts, entire walls of graffiti, and posters bear his resemblance, but they're for tourists to take home and dream about.

Like all humans, Cubans yearn for the opportunity to live a better material life. Yoli, our energetic guide on this my second trip to the island, has ambitions to start her own business, possibly dwell in an open Scandinavian country and make money. When she was young, her family practiced Santería, the pantheistic African Yoruba religion mixing African gods with Catholic saints. The Santería practices continue throughout Cuba, accepted by the Castro regime. Yoli no longer follows these practices. She's well educated, fashionably dressed, strong, and brilliant at solving her visitors' problems.

"Most Cubans are more interested in sharing something with you than getting something from you. They are unmoved by talk of your material accomplishments," travel writer Christopher Baker observed in his Moon Guide, *Cuba*. Baker commented further that Cubans don't fear physical contact; they lean into visitors in a very human way. And they commit themselves to social justice as a national belief.

Gabriel García Márquez says it best in *One Hundred Years of Solitude*. "One minute of reconciliation is worth more than a whole life of friendship."

Cuban band playing in an open-air building

Finding My Coda to Buena Vista Social Club
Carol J. Kelly

"They do it for money." Our local guide was emphatic in her assessment of Havana's current crop of musicians. Cuban bands don't play for the love of music, she says flatly, nor do they play to entertain other Cubans. These bands proliferate in Havana's bars, nightclubs, hotel lobbies, town squares and street corners because the city is the top destination for foreigners, and musicians perform primarily for tips from tourists. "And most of these bands aren't even that good," she adds.

Like most tourists, I came to Cuba thinking music is deep within the soul of the island—in the blood of its people, and an integral part of the country's history. I come from Jamaica where reggae is king. Music styles like *Son Cubano*, I felt, were so embedded in the culture that singing or playing an instrument was the norm, not just for *Habaneros*, but for Cubans in every corner of the land. I knew that our guide's perspective was true for her, but it seemed a bit cynical to peg Havana's musicians as mostly mercenary. Perhaps something shifted after decades of economic hardship and in more recent lean years. Beyond the music popularized by the Buena Vista Social Club, I knew very little about Cuban music. So, with hardly any preconceived notions in my way, I decided to tune in, listen up, and find out for myself what was really going on in Cuba's music scene. I wondered how tourists like me played into the choices of true artists, whose music springs from the heart.

"There's a little bit of Congo in every Cuban," is a popular saying that acknowledges the African roots of music, art and culture. I can feel the truth of this saying deep in my bones from the moment I land. My first night happens to be a Friday—party night in Havana—and everyone is poised for pleasure. Having just escaped winter in New York, I am ready for the warmth of the Caribbean, the vibrancy and rich diversity of its people, and most of all, for the pulsating rhythms of traditional Cuban music. *Son Cubano*, the genre of mountain music and dance revitalized globally by the ensemble called the Buena Vista Social Club, saturates the air because its lush, lavish, Latin beat is what tourists want to hear. I hear and see bands in almost every bar, lounge and restaurant as we walk the narrow streets of Old Havana on our way to dinner near the Malecón.

Turning a corner, we see a small group of musicians rehearsing at an outdoor table; a young boy is spontaneously dancing in the street. At NaO, the restaurant where my fellow writers and I have our first meal, a lively band called Nuevo Son performs the romantic, traditional music next to our table. It's a joy to hear the distinctive Cuban tres guitar, a key ingredient of *son's* magic sauce, exquisitely played by a musician who looks to be in his seventies. The much-younger lead singer, a real showman, encourages diners to clap and sing along, call-and-response style. On a break, he drums up tips and even issues a charming call to action: "Buy our CD!" Many in our group gladly paid the ten CUCs (ten dollars) to take the captivating music of Nuevo Son home with us.

Near Kingston, Jamaica, where I grew up—about 500 miles south of Havana—music was, and still is, an integral part of our culture. I was used to hearing loud music blaring on every street corner until the wee hours of the morning, but it came though sound systems —boom boxes, records and tapes—not from live performances by bands.

Jamaica, the birthplace of reggae, has a culture of listeners, not performers—recorded music rather than live music. I rarely saw live bands unless it was a special event, a major fundraiser, or a scheduled concert. It's never as spontaneous as it is in Cuba. Generally, Jamaican restaurants, bars and nightclubs still play records, CDs, or have DJs who select from thousands of downloaded songs on laptops. Bob Marley, who died in 1981, was and still is Jamaica's global evangelist of traditional reggae. Similarly, the Buena Vista Social Club became the face of *Son Cubano*, re-popularizing this enchantingly lyrical, old-fashioned style of music on the world stage in the late 1990s.

Of course, in preparation for my trip to Cuba, I watched *Buena Vista Social Club*, the award-winning 1999 documentary about the band. The film features veteran, almost-forgotten musicians, including Ibrahim Ferrer on vocals and Rubén González on piano, performing *son* songs filled with longing and romance. *Son* originated in the eastern Cuba in the 19th century, blending Spanish and African influences. It had an international presence before the 1959 Revolution, during the island's big-band nightclub era, when Cuban musicians toured abroad. When stars like Frank Sinatra, Nat "King" Cole, Josephine Baker and Desi Arnaz (and alter ego Ricky Ricardo singing Babalú) graced venues such as Hotel Nacional, *son* was part of the soundtrack for Mafia-backed gambling and prostitution, big stage shows, and big Hollywood luminaries. After the Revolution, corrupt activities linked to the mob came to a halt, and the big band era was muted. But the socialist regime started an excellent system of free music education.

After that first Friday night in Havana and throughout my weeklong trip, a feeling of excitement, anticipation and pure pleasure would flood my body listening to different versions of *son* staples like "Quizas, Quizas," "El Carretero," and "Candela." On Saturday night, our local guide arranges a treat—she gets us into Fabrica de Arte Cubano, an ultra-hip nightclub/art gallery in Vedado, about a half-hour cab ride from our *casa particular*. A live band performs in the outdoor space, while DJ music pulsates inside: hip-hop, rap, R&B, rumba, reggaetón, salsa, timba and South American dance hits. Of course, it doesn't take long to hear and feel the full blast of Luis Fonsi's "Despacito," the 2017 global smash from Puerto Rico. And though I don't hit the actual dance floor, the music fills me up, piercing my heart and soul as I rock and march in step with it, revelling in the atmosphere and the glorious diversity of the crowd.

Regular street parties amplify Havana's musical heartbeat. Rumba, a deeply rooted, complex Afro-Cuban genre of popular music, fills the air at Callejon de Hamel every Sunday around noon. Luckily, our group gets to experience the outdoor carnival atmosphere of "*La rumba de Cayo Hues*" in glorious weather. (It had rained the day before.) Rumba singers, dancers and drummers captivate a diverse crowd of locals and tourists on streets, lined with art galleries and artsy bars. The percussive beats of bongo drums, congas, cowbells, claves and sticks cast a spell on the performers, the crowd and me. Driven by the rumba-infused warmth of the moment, inhibitions slide, and everyone is dancing. And though I didn't get lost in the music, I was keeping the beat and swinging in place. Of course, the *rumberos* took breaks from their frenzied singing and dancing to ask for tips. And a friendly young couple with a baby started pleading with my companion and me for money. The symbolic meaning of the dance and its links to Santería religious traditions went way over my head, but I later learned that the rumba was born in the poor neighborhoods of Matanzas in the north—also in the late 19th century—with roots in African music. They say Cuba is sugar cane, rum and rumba—if you understand these three, you understand the island. I was definitely getting it.

I got the sense that Cuban children, unlike Jamaican kids, are encouraged to develop themselves musically. It seems so organic. From a very young age, Cuban children listen to family members and friends playing solo or in bands and aspire to perform themselves. And most of them learn to play an instrument, even if it's only hitting two sticks together. Some lucky children make it to music schools, including Instituto Superior de Arte (ISA), Havana's most prestigious conservatory. Only children who show a special interest in music and pass an aptitude test may be admitted, and their rigorous education is free. The problem though is, once they're trained, it's hard to make a living.

"I don't see a future for Cuban music," said bandleader Amaranda Fernandez, who was celebrating his ninetieth birthday the day I met him by chance at Café Viales on my way to an elusive Internet hotspot. Through a translator, he continued: "I think in the past we had more opportunities to go to other countries to perform, which was very well paid compared to what we make here." Amaranda said there are many music schools in Cuba, but not many places to perform. Furthermore, musicians' hopes for a big tourist boom and more gigs were dashed by the current U.S. administration's reversal of President Obama's initiative to restore relations with Cuba and open up investment.

That explains why musicians in Havana have to hustle. They're also competing with part-time, occasional musicians who have other careers or jobs. Making money is a driving force because college-educated professionals earn very little in Cuba. Moonlighting in the tourist industry—playing in a band, driving a taxi, or becoming a tour guide—are ways to augment meager state salaries, so tips are tempting for most Cubans, particularly *Habaneros*. Since most Cubans can sing or play music, it makes perfect sense that they play in bands to earn extra money from tips.

Amaranda, a pianist and keyboardist, has been a professional musician for almost seventy years and has seen a lot of changes. He feels lucky to still be working at his age. To hear Amaranda tell it, he was there when the Buena Vista Social Club was just a notion, doing solo gigs with different band members, some of whom have died. He was touring in South America when American guitarist Ry Cooder and Cuban bandleader Juan de Marcos González were recording and shooting in Cuba. "The traditional Cuban music is a very important legacy," says Amaranda, "and *son* is the base for other rhythms like *musica popular bailable* (popular dance music). Buena Vista Social Club made that sound very popular around the world, and here in Cuba as well."

Mitchell, a waiter at the Old Havana café where Amaranda's band plays, tells me that for Cubans, music is "normal." The Cuban people "with a glass and spoon and plate can make music. It's in our blood—in every place."

What kind music do young Cubans like? They don't necessarily listen to *son* and rumba, favoring reggaetón, hip-hop, rap, salsa and other newer Latin rhythms. But everyone respects traditional *son*, rumba, mambo, cha-cha-cha, dengué, contra and wawanco. When I asked a cool, young, Cuban woman what kind of music she likes, she said college-educated people enjoy a genre called "*cancion inteligente*," or smart song, popularized by musicians like Pablo Milanés,

Silvo Rodriguez and Jorge Drexler. She's not one of the *reggaetoneros*, because she finds reggaetón too boring. You could say that reggaetón is reggae's stepchild: Though reggaetón is derived from Jamaican reggae, its beat is faster and more insistent, it's strongly influenced by American hip-hop, and almost always has Spanish lyrics. Perhaps young Cubans love reggaetón largely because young people everywhere love hip-hop.

Did I spot any musical hustlers during my weeklong visit? *Quizás.* (Maybe.) In my view, neither true musicians nor poorly paid professionals have the freedom to choose how to earn a living in Cuba's harsh economy. Moonlighting is a fact of life.

In Cuba, I found a musical culture deeply rooted in the island's links to Africa, Spain and Latin America. I saw the joy of jam sessions, of musicians improvising and trading riffs while singing generations-old songs of love and longing. I could feel the energy between the audience and band members in both formal and informal venues. I even participated; at La Taberna, a Havana nightclub featuring *son* and other traditional music, I joined the conga line and danced onstage. It's tough to make good music without passion, or with corrupt intent. In fact, it's almost impossible. To reach an audience, to truly move them, musicians have to share something authentic, something coming from deep inside.

Yes, they do it for money. Musicians need to eke out a living and often play for tips from tourists. But in my experience with Cuban bands, and judging from the joyful feeling I got listening and dancing to them, they also do it for love.

Cuban dancers at an outdoor event

¡Bailemos!
Donna Hemmila

The furious pounding of claves and congas crashes over the crowd like sea-storm waves, and I am diving in. It's a blustery Sunday night in Trinidad at the open-air Casa de la Música dance hall, possibly the best place to sweat and swagger to authentic salsa in all of Cuba.

I've spent the last four days listening to Cuban music, visiting cultural centers and taking dance lessons—all designed to pump my heart—and feet—full of fiery Latin beats. I'm now ready for my grand finale.

Rumba. Mambo. Salsa. I've danced them all. There's just one more Cuban-born dance on my list, the cha cha cha. When its drunken rhythms start to play, my dance partner pulls me out of my seat.

"Let's do it," Reinier says.

"*¡Bailemos!*" I agree. "Let's dance."

We start with the basics: one, two, one, two, three, back, forward, cha, cha, cha. We do a few side-to-side steps and half turns. Then I whirl into a full turn. That's when I realize we are the only ones dancing. For whatever reason, the hundreds of locals and tourists gathered here tonight have chosen to take a break. Should we sit down? Pretend I've twisted an ankle and slink off in shame? Not happening.

For one brief shining moment, I am Queen of the Prom, dancing in the spotlight with the perfect partner. If I have not completely mastered every step and pivot, I have at least fully embraced the Cuban spirit of dancing like no one is watching. Only in this case, everyone is watching.

At the end of our solitary cha cha, Reinier slaps a two-handed high five on me, and a few in the audience applaud. Once again Reinier assures me I am a good dancer. I take his compliments with the same polite appreciation I display when he tells me *mi acento españole es bueno*, when clearly it is not. We're an odd pair: he, a tall, thirty-something Afro-Cuban, and I, a white American grandmother, twice his age and a foot and a half shorter. Sometimes people stare, perhaps not guessing that I've hired him to dance with me.

A former Internet engineer, Reinier Luaces is one of the many young, highly educated, entrepreneurial Cubans who now earn a living as a tourist guide, a job more profitable than government work. Locally Sourced, the company our writing group engaged for our Havana sojourn, promised me a good dancer for my extended one-person tour. Reinier did not disappoint. He is not only a good dancer, but a man who loves to dance, a rarity among my circle of American males. I think of all the men I've known whose dance experiences consist of prom night and that one required dance at their daughter's wedding. As I have learned, that's not the Cuban way.

To explain how I know this, I must start at the beginning. My dance adventure began in Havana at Café Taberna, a nightclub where the Wanderland Writers enjoyed their last night together before heading home or going off on solo Cuban excursions. The club features two professional dancers who perform with a Big Band dance orchestra reminiscent of the days when mambo was king and Benny Moré was out-crooning Frank Sinatra. At points in the performance, the dancers invite audience members to join them. When the male dancer beckoned, I leapt from my seat. Thanks to years of Zumba classes, I knew enough mambo steps to fake it.

At the end of the night, the dancers started a conga line, and everyone in the club, even the shyest of my fellow writers, joined the human chain as it snaked around the room. In this dance, each person holds onto the shoulders of the one in front, swaying in unison to the da-da-da-boom drumbeat.

Conga is the first Latin dance I learned. In the 1950s, Cuban music surged in popularity in the United States. I credit Ricky Ricardo, the fictitious Cuban bandleader Desi Arnaz portrayed in the *I Love Lucy* TV sit-com. Nearly every episode featured Arnaz singing and pounding his conga drum. This captivated my father.

Every Christmas Eve, my Polish family gathered at Uncle Mickey and Aunt Irene's house to celebrate. Without fail, after Dad had consumed too much vodka, he'd call out "everybody form a conga line." Not exactly a Hallmark holiday memory, but one that I cherish.

In the time warp in which much of Cuba operates, I was delighted to see people at Café Taberna still forming conga lines. I took this as a sign that my dance quest would bear fruit.

The next morning, Reinier and our driver, Leandro, picked me up in a '92 Peugeot, and we headed to Matanzas, the birthplace of the rumba. Once known as the Athens of Cuba for its cultural vibrancy, Matanzas lies an hour's drive outside of Havana. Doomed to exist in the shadow of Veradero, the nearby seaside tourist resort, Matanzas fails to attract many foreigners, despite its thriving bohemian art scene. So my desire for a rumba lesson in the town where rumba sprang to life was not a common one. We arrived in town still searching for a rumba master. Luckily, Maria, the host of our *casa particular,* knew a guy.

That is how things get done in Cuba. Someone, somewhere will always know a guy or lady who can get you what you're looking for. In my case, it was rumba teacher Alexis Morales O'Farrill, a former dancer with the National Folkloric Company of Cuba, who now serves as president of a dance festival, as a percussion and voice teacher and as a choreographer.

Alexis also gives nightly dance lessons to local teenagers at the Matanzas cultural center to keep them off the streets and to preserve traditional Cuban dance.

Every Cuban dance teacher I meet will have the same complaint: Kids today only care about *reggaeton*. This mix of reggae and hip-hop music carries the same taint of violence and crude lyrics that dogs our own American hip-hop culture.

When we arrived at the cultural center, a decaying colonial edifice with peeling paint, cracked tiles and a spacious dance studio, eight Matanzas teenagers were waiting to dance with Alexis. I said I didn't mind if they hung out while I had my lesson. Alexis cautioned them to pay attention and learn from what he was about to show me.

The basic rumba steps are simple. It's the sensuous, undulating hip and arm movements that turn easy footwork into rumba. I tried my best to emulate the female dancer tasked with demonstrating the woman's steps for me.

After running through the basics, we stopped for an explanation of the next part of the dance, which had something to do with inoculations. Wait, what? Was the teacher worried I hadn't had my flu shot?

"Think of an inoculator," Reinier attempted to explain. "The man is the plunger and the woman is the receiver of the inoculation." Many hand gestures accompanied this translation until I understood what was required.

In this step sequence, the man shoots a hand forward toward the woman's privates. The woman, in response, demurely places a hand over said privy parts to decline the *inoculation*. She then blows the man a flirty kiss. Or she can flip her hand in a brushing-off signal. The man can also deliver the shot with a lighting-quick kick of his foot toward the woman's private parts. This pantomime, I was told, signals the man's interest in the young lady. She covers her nether region to let her family and neighbors know she's just not that kind of girl.

At first, Alexis alerted me to the musical count at which he would inoculate me. That gave me a fighting chance to protect my virtue. Symbolically, of course. The man never actually touches the woman *down there*.

After a while, Alexis decided it was more fun to throw the gesture in when I'd least expect it. I was seldom quick enough to get my hand in the right place at the right time. When I did, I looked like a toddler who has to pee, knees together and hands clapped tightly over my privates.

At times, Alexis stooped to trickery. He'd feign wiping his sweaty brow, pretending to take a break from the dancing. Then he'd whirl around to deliver a foot kick or hand jab. Another time he gallantly took my arm in his to execute a forward strut-step common in salsa. Then his hand flew out like a cobra striking its prey. Once again, I was too slow to prevent the symbolic incursion into my lady parts. Everyone so enjoyed my ineptitude that I didn't have the heart to declare enough is enough. At the end of my lesson, I got to dance with the older boys and take group selfies. Secretly, I wished I could have danced a bit of *reggaeton* with them.

The next morning, driver Leandro dropped Reiner and me in Trinidad, further south and on the opposite coast from Havana and

Matanzas. In this vibrant, pastel-painted colonial city, I had two more dance lessons, starting with the mambo.

The lesson took place in a private house, the street-level foyer of which doubles as a dance studio. A small Santería altar to the Virgin Mary stood in a corner. I silently asked for her assistance in not looking like an idiot during the lesson to come.

A cloudburst had turned the street out front into a river of rushing water, delaying my mambo instructor's arrival. While we waited, Reinier and I watched a young Russian ballerina work on a choreographed number with hip lifts and complicated turn patterns. While she rehearsed with her teacher, another instructor arrived with two college-aged Asian men. Judging by their shy awkwardness, they were experiencing their first salsa lesson. Amazingly, after only an hour, the two young men learned enough to go dancing.

When Yusley Despaigne Escobar, professor of dance, arrived, the first thing he did was remove his red high-top canvas shoes and dry his feet. He'd had to wade through the flooded street to get to me. Yusley used to be a medical doctor but makes a better living teaching dance. He gives six to eight lessons a day, sometimes teaching ten hours, such is the world's hunger for Cuban dance.

He taught me a simple routine punctuated with quick foot kicks and swivels. It would takes years of daily training to reach the level of the performers I saw in Havana, but the Santería Virgin worked her magic. Inwardly, I congratulated myself for my mad skills, not knowing that the hardest dance lesson was yet to come.

We met up with Iory Rossell Suárez del Villar on the second floor terrace of a restaurant. First, Iory offered cups of strong Cuban coffee. After this polite formality, the tough taskmaster within her emerged.

"First I test you," Iory said.

A pop quiz in salsa?

"I have to see what you know," she explained.

Cue music.

I danced the basic salsa steps with the male dancer tapped to lead me through my paces. I passed Level 1. Yes! But before the lesson could commence in earnest, more hurdles had to be cleared. Turns and cross-body patterns. I gave it all I had. When the music ended, Iory proclaimed me Level 6. I asked Reiner how many levels there were.

"I'm sure there are only ten," he said reassuringly. If that were true, and not merely more encouraging politeness, I rank as an intermediate-level amateur salsa dancer. Lack of technique or talent should never keep anyone off the dance floor, but a little basic knowledge doesn't hurt. I felt ready to put all I'd learned together for one memorable night on the town.

When I asked Cubans where they learned to dance, they answered with puzzled expressions. Most, even the professionals, said they learned from their mothers. Reinier had another answer. "We're born dancing," he said. To prove it, he showed me a cellphone video of his three-year-old daughter busting some serious moves to a music video playing on the TV.

Born dancing, Cubans, I suspect, leave this world the same way.

At the Casa de la Música, Reinier and I danced next to an elderly couple, one of the best pairs on the floor. They recognized us from a visit we'd made that afternoon to the Trinidad cultural center to watch a youth dance lesson. They had been hanging paper streamers in the hall. "We've been dancing since three o'clock," the woman told us with a laugh. It was after nine when Reinier and I called it a night, and they were still moving to the music, sparks still smoldering between them.

They were old enough to have lived through the Revolution and the Special Period of extreme hardship and hunger after the Soviets withdrew aid to Cuba. Yet, no matter what they have or don't have—most in Cuba have very little—this couple seemed to possess wealth unimaginable. They epitomize the spirit of dance I came to Cuba to experience—that which makes life bearable in dark times and glorious in times of joy and celebration.

That is how my Cuban dance journey ended: dancing with the perfect partner, next to an elderly couple swaying to the same beat on a blustery night in Trinidad.

I think of them whenever I feel like dancing.

Camilo Cienfuegos and Fidel Castro played for the Barbudos.

At the Crack of the Bat

MJ Pramik

"*Crack!*" My heart skips two beats. No, three. That rocket sound says it's a goner. Over the left field fence, high and deep. Then: total bedlam. A twenty-five-piece live ensemble gyrates and hoots, blaring their trumpets; and pulsing congas, steel drums, a grand bass and all variety of percussion instruments rev up the crowd. This Cuban rhythm troupe emphatically outclasses the canned techno music I'm used to hearing at the San Francisco Giants' stadium. They have us dancing in the stands.

Nothing satisfies like a solid home run. Bottom of the second inning, the Havana Industriales' hulking, six-foot-five player number sixty-nine sent a beauty over the left field fence in this game against Las Tunas.

I'm jumping up and down in Estadio Latinoamericano at the first game of Cuba's 2017 National Series. It's nighttime in Havana's Cerro neighborhood. I was drafted to accompany my friend Rufus, a cricket player from northeast of London, who direly needed some womansplaining about American baseball. We arrive early and score perfect seats behind home plate. The stadium accommodates 55,000 but tonight's attendance runs low, as, I surmised, few in Havana can afford the three-dollar entry fee.

Rufus and I merge through the gates and past guards amid an overwhelmingly friendly crowd. Smiles, thumbs ups, affable nods; everybody's friends at a baseball game. Glancing about, we joked that health authorities certainly don't patrol the food service areas here under the stands. Roasted pork sandwiches, sliced off a rotating spit by a fellow in a white chef's hat, would tantalize anyone at twice the price. Dogs ramble throughout the lower level food court, patrolling for tidbits. An outgoing, good-looking Cuban fan poses for photos holding aloft four pork sandwiches in one hand. They smell gorgeous: smoked meat and zesty spices. My mouth waters at this mix of aromas, piquant colors and intense public excitement.

We watch the game from the stands, screened by a flopping net to keep us safe from pop flies. I explain the nuances of baseball rules—essentially what the players are doing—while Rufus notes some vague parallels to cricket. Granted, cricket and baseball are bat-and-ball games, but a baseball diamond differs dramatically from the cricket field's usual elliptical shape. For instance, I am amazed to learn that a cricket field's fair territory can be 50 percent bigger than the baseball diamond right in front of me.

This Wednesday night in Havana, the hitters hit, the catchers catch, the pitchers pitch, but alas, our home team loses four to three in this first game of the three-set series for the 2017 Cuban National Series (akin to the World Series in the United States).

Later, the Industriales went on to lose the series in just two games. Perhaps they missed the spirit of their Number-One Fan, Armando Luis Torres, better known as Armandito "El Tintorero." He'd worked for a dry cleaner; *tintorero* means dryer, hence the nickname. Also called "Show Man," El Tintorero, an orphan, found a family among the Industriales and had attended every one of their games since 1968. Accompanied by his dog, Pillo Chocolate, El Tintorero led the wildly cheering fans from his bench seat at third base. When he died in 2004, the team placed a bronze statue of their beloved fan in this seat so he'd never miss a game. He sits there across the stands from where Rufus and I watched.

The Industriales' blue and white uniform is sacred to Cuban ballplayers. Many Cuban boys aspire to play for the team one day. Even rival team members have confessed to this career dream. The Industriales are duly celebrated for being the most successful Cuban National League team of all time; they're also beloved simply because they're from the capital of Cuba.

Many of their players have gone on to international careers. Major League Baseball pitcher Orlando "El Duque" Hernández pitched for the Industriales in Havana and the Cuban National team in international play, then defected to the United States in 1997 and pitched for the New York Yankees, Chicago White Sox, Arizona Diamondbacks and New York Mets during his time in the Majors. With the Yankees, he won three World Series rings. Even this great (some call him magical) player once admitted he always wore his Industriales jersey under his New York Yankees uniform.

With "El Duque" in mind, I buy the blue and white cap for my six-year-old grandson, who's now in love with the sport.

After the game, Rufus and I wander through the Cerro area searching for a taxi. Street food aromas mix with the dense Havana night air. The area, dark and desolate, seems abandoned. Finally, we flag down an idle red- and black-painted cab with an interior that smells of auto exhaust and grease. The driver chatters on about baseball as we drive thirty minutes across town to our *casa particular.*

Over a thank-you beer from Rufus at the *casa's* makeshift rooftop bar, I recall my own early passion for the game, remembering my father with one ear on a baseball game on the radio, one eye on the black-and-white TV's diamond on the screen, and one eye asleep from so many hours in the coal mine. Some Sundays I'd join him to watch the Pittsburgh Pirates or the Cleveland Indians spar with their respective division teams. I loved the Pirates and held the Indians in high regard (being from Ohio), but secretly rooted for the New York Yankees. This last fact I never spoke out loud.

It was family lore that my father competed in local baseball when I was an infant. Agile and fleet, he played shortstop. I've saved one *Martin's Ferry Times Leader* sports page cutting, now yellow after decades: "Pramik Saves League Play Off!" He had an offer to try out for the Detroit Tigers before World War II, but family needs held him back. My mother proudly recounted that during his Marine Corps service, and before he shipped out of San Diego, his Semper Fi! platoon played a pickup game in San Diego against the U.S. Navy and their slugger Joe DiMaggio.

In Cuba, the diamond sport still reigns supreme. Twenty-two-year-old first baseman Leonel Segura Morales, who plays for the Camaguey Alfareros, told me in a translated interview that he's played baseball since age seven.

"I play baseball because when I was a little boy I remember the first present I got was a bat and a baseball. It was when my grandfather started playing with me and I fell in love with the game. Here the students can choose which sport they want to practice as an extra school activity, and I started playing baseball. We used to practice almost every day."

He added: "I think I like baseball because of my grandpa. And also since baseball's the national sport in Cuba, I saw people playing on the streets and the game became part of me since I was a little boy."

Cubans can now regularly watch baseball on television.

"We get more information about what's happening in the world," said Morales. "Soccer is at the moment the sport that seems to play the most on TV, but when we have the opportunity to watch baseball, everyone forgets about soccer. It is part of us, part of our idiosyncrasy."

As an official member of a national team, he earns about 950 Cuban pesos (CUPs; currently equivalent to $35.85 U.S.) a month before deductions through the Instituto Nacional de Deporte y Recreación (National Institute for Sports and Recreation). When a team wins the national series, it receives about 60,000 CUPs, which is shared among the players.

When asked about the heroes of Cuban baseball, Segura Morales gave an astonishing answer.

"The first one of all is Fidel Castro." He went on to name others, such as Martin Dihigo, known as "El Maestro," considered one of the best players of all time, master of fastball and curve ball hitting; and Miguel Cuevas, infielder and outfielder who hit three home runs in the 1963 Pan American Games when Cuba won the gold medal.

But it is Fidel Castro who interests me. His love of baseball is legendary—he wanted to share in the life of the Cuban people, and for them to know he was a fellow Cuban. Although, contrary to legend, he neither tried out for, nor was drafted by the New York Yankees, as a politician, Castro used baseball as part of Cuban politics. Los Barbudos (the Bearded Ones), Castro's baseball team composed of fellow Revolutionaries, played before exhibition games during professional seasons. In pre-Revolutionary times, Cubans believe that Castro and other plotters attended baseball games throughout the country, sitting anonymously in the stands as a cover, while hatching plans against Batista's dictatorship.

Castro believed that access to sport and recreation was a human right, that exercise would support each Cuban citizen and promote a sound body and a strong mind. Castro's attitude about sports also applied to music, dance, art and culture. All a child had to bring was aptitude and attitude.

During the Cold War and before la Revolución and Castro's rise, Cuban-born baseball players would play in the American Negro Leagues and in Major League Baseball. After the Revolution, many Cuban players defected to the United States. This split families, since the Cuban government would not grant exit visas for spouses or children of some players.

Then, after the 1991 Russian exit and so-called "Special Period" of deep economic despair, the Cuban government branded baseball defectors as disloyal, which only led to more defections. The government stopped "El Duque," who initially remained loyal to Cuba, from playing for the national team after his half-brother Liván Hernández defected in 1995. After two years of repression, Orlando followed his brother to the United States.

Wishful Americans and Cubans alike have attempted poignant efforts to use baseball to bridge relations between the two countries. In March, 1999, Cuba played the Baltimore Orioles (Orioles won three to two) in an exhibition game in Havana. A few months later, the Cuban national team beat the Orioles in Baltimore (Cuba won twelve to six) in the second of the series. These games marked the first time the Cuban national team took on the all-major-league players, and the first time since 1959 that Major League Baseball hit the diamond on Cuban soil. The ambassador and instigator of this series was Peter Angelos, owner of the Baltimore Orioles. He lobbied the U.S. government and President Bill Clinton to hold this cultural exchange.

John Angelos, chief operating officer of the Baltimore Orioles, gave an interview with Dave Zirin in *The Nation* magazine in December 2016, making his own comparison between Cuban baseball prowess and that of other countries: "Cuba is 11 million people, which is about the same size as the Dominican Republic, and has also produced a lot of baseball players. But Cuba, in terms of Olympic medals in baseball, and the international World Cup (World Baseball Classic), has excelled. On a per capital basis, when you look at all sports, there are many, many times the medals per person than most countries, including the United States."

Angelos most likely had in mind the national Cuban baseball hero Frederich Cepeda Cruz. The 38-year-old outfielder played on the Cuban team when they won the gold medal in the 2004 Summer Olympics, the silver medal in the 2008 Summer Olympics, and, in the 2009 World Baseball Classic, had a .500 batting average, three homers in six games in twenty-four at-bats. In 2014, he joined the Yomiiuri Giants of Nippon Professional Baseball after salary-ceiling restrictions were dropped for Cubans playing in the Major Leagues.

Or, as Segura Morales put it: "Cuban baseball is part of the people, their way of living; it makes us happy and torments us as well. Sometimes the athletes make their own materials [such as bases, balls]. The playing and the training conditions are very different to other countries and yet we have achieved important awards internationally. The greatest motivation for a Cuban baseball player is the fans. We don't play for money because we hardly make any money playing. It's all about the heart and pride in our team."

I contemplate the passion inspired by baseball while walking across Havana's Parque Central. Men of all ages gesture and shout, discussing the national sport—hits, runs and advice on the game and life. Through a friend I learned Industriales' number sixty-nine is Eriel Sanchez when she checked in at *la esquina caliente* (the hot corner). Boisterous, animated, they dress in suits, exercise outfits or shorts and sandals and attract passersby. I feel the pull to join the debate with my *muy poco* Spanish skills. Knowing better, I keep walking.

Segura Morales' baseball pronouncements strike a chord with me. My family's love of baseball now spans generations and runs through grandson Henry's love of the sport. I watch his T-ball games in San Diego and the videos my daughter posts of him playing. He's focused, primed, ready like his Great-Grandpa Joe. I smile, imaging him wearing his Havana Industriales cap under his navy-blue helmet as he swings for his team, the Padres.

Woman in Camagüey

Camagüey with Me
Tania Amochaev

I am seated in a restaurant on the lively plaza in the heart of Camagüey, Cuba, sipping an after-dinner drink. I've tabled my camera and, turning my head, I'm taking in the whole, unedited scene.

Old lamps send a warm glow onto dark skin. Sculpted bodies parade with an ease that makes San Francisco puritan in contrast. Then she appears. Bold red pants cup her impossibly curved buttocks. Endless legs lead down into tall heels that somehow click rather than clunk. Dancing hips pull up, up, and up, through the swaying movements of generous breasts to the brief gleam of a dark, smiling face. A swish of long hair flashes as she disappears into the crowd, all eyes following in hope of one more glimpse.

Camagüey, pronounced Come-away—as in "come away with me"—calls to me still to come away to its allure, its mazed streets, its art, and its beautiful women. My own art took a significant leap forward in those streets. It was in attempting to capture the magic of Camagüey that I finally understood that my iPhone is the only camera I need.

As I walk past an ancient doorway, a gaunt, timeworn woman gazes at me, at first with nervous tension, a moment later relaxed, not minding that I take a photograph. As I look at it today, I see her curiosity, her thinning skin, the details of the darkness she sits in, the knitting on the shawl over the seat of an old carved wooden chair. My lack of a giant camera prevents intimidation, the push-button ease-of-use helps me capture exactly the spirit I see and feel. And my focus on her soul rather than on sophisticated technology starts me on a path that still gives me great joy.

"Camagüey, quaintest and least known of Cuban cities, is a storehouse of delight to the casual visitor and a source of undying joy to the man behind the camera, for in Camagüey the sixteenth century clasps hands with the twentieth, across streets so narrow that each carriage driver should possess a pilot's license to navigate them in safety."

This description, written in 1905 by Elisa Armstrong Bengough, could be adapted to my own visit by simply replacing the man with a woman and the twentieth century with the twenty-first. The streets might be a little wider, and the buildings more decrepit, but a wide walking plaza now links two neighborhoods, with some seating, shops and cafes slowly sprouting along its length.

In the early dawn, as most people sleep, the street sweepers mingle with a few cats. Years of habit see me up and about. The glint of well-worn cobblestones pulls me along to a bread hawker setting up his cart. I breathe in the aroma of fresh loaves and anticipate his seductive wake-up calls. The street hawkers' carts are an early clue to the artistic nature of this town. Like in other cities, decrepit three-wheeled wooden vehicles are constantly pushed along streets where few cars interfere with their passage. These carts are artfully decorated with garlic strands hanging just so and onions sorted by size and color

The pulse of life is somehow gentler here than in other parts of Cuba, as if the very environment is telling me to slow down, look around, enjoy. The pedicabs burst with colorful, bold and unique designs. People sell flowers on the street—often plastic, but beautiful.

Art is scattered widely. And not just the pervasive, institutionalized revolutionary statues that grace every central square throughout this land.

In one square that I visit the sculptress Martha Jiménez has positioned bronze women exhibiting rolls of fat that might embarrass, but instead are shown off, as they are by humans all around me. I envision her unique sculpted fountain in my yard, featuring an irresistibly laughing, well-endowed, nearly naked woman—bent in a manner that would have my thighs screaming—the healthy stream of her urine permanently watering what lies underneath. Almost alive, she gazes at me with a "Why are you staring at me?" gleam in her eyes.

How can I resist? I, who travel with only carry-on luggage whether for two days or two months, haul home a crate that holds Oscar Lasseria's large and fanciful three-dimensional painting displaying breasts that could quiet any baby's crying. The women's hair is made of plastic spoons and forks; the colors are bold and outrageous, as is the tilt of their breasts. I grin as I stare at it over my morning coffee.

It must be something about the aura of this town that leads to sensuous women in life as in art. And the sassiness seems to start young and last long. I walk past four little girls sitting in a windowsill the width of two women's bottoms. As I focus on the scene, they instantly adopt poses that were surely learned from the seductive sexiness of older sisters. Nearby, a much older woman pulls me in to show me pictures of her granddaughters, displayed on a wall whose ancient texture I would pay dearly to replicate in my own bedroom. Around eighty for certain, she still wears clothing more revealing than anything I own.

These memories feel more poignant when I return to Cuba to spend a week in Havana, just absorbing its atmosphere. My own country is struggling with leadership that feels repressive and a growing awareness that women are not getting an even chance.

My guide on the current trip is a young woman named Yoli. Amazingly, she lives in Camagüey. Yoli, as befits a sophisticated tour leader, is far more demurely attired than my memory of the women in Camagüey. But as I keep staring at her gorgeous face, her lovely figure, I wonder if she isn't one of the beautiful women I observed walking through the squares of that town.

She could well have been the one who inspired my rapture, for she is beautiful in body, soul and spirit. No request is too challenging, whether it is an interview with a baseball team or a visit to the spiritual burning of an idol. Early in the morning or late at night, her smile glows in the nascent light as she shares her knowledge with over-privileged strangers who keep trying to dig deeper into her psyche and that of her homeland.

Yoli could leave Cuba to find a better life in America; her independent spirit would thrive in our country. But she wants to stay and help her homeland move into the future. I don't know if I could love a land enough to make that kind of sacrifice. My own life in the United States has allowed a success unimaginable in Cuba. But my background as an immigrant from a communist country—one who left not long before Yoli's country fought its way through its own revolution—leaves me happy to have evaded that choice.

Yoli's country should be grateful for her determination to stay and make a difference. It should recognize her and all the women who nourish their land, women who impressed me with their resilience and their strength yet disturbed me with their political invisibility.

Like all other Cuban cities, Camagüey's main squares are anchored with statues of its revolutionary leaders. "Never forget" might as well still be plastered everywhere. And how could anyone forget? It seems to me that these famous heroes—these men—displayed in the squares of every town, brought a revolution that shattered but has yet to reach the stage of rebuilding. One that talked of equality for women but left behind mostly decrepit broken buildings and dead men frozen in bronze to grace the hearts of city squares. One that empowered the few and impoverished the rest. They set off a revolution that blazed more fiercely than fireworks but fizzled into a state that would lead a less resilient people into despair.

Yet the women of Cuba walk tall and proud, and once more I am torn between the joys of walking through this world that hasn't evolved much in sixty years and my anger at the men in power who help keep it that way.

My thoughts inevitably return to that night in Camagüey's Rooster Square, named for the large image of that animal on a building nearby. To the mojitos. To sitting and drinking. To watching the passersby. To the procession of sexy women whose firm breasts have coaxed me into walking taller and jutting my own ample but well hidden bosom out a bit more. Into swaying my butt a bit, as perhaps I should have those many years ago when I was their age.

And again she appears before me. She is a unique beauty; she is all the women I have seen and heard in Cuba.

Hers is the sculpture that, if placed in town squares, would energize a new era better than any dead revolutionary hero. Hers is the body and heart that will expand and nurture Cuba's next generation and produce more men like my Cuban friend Martin, whose first and deepest love is unabashedly reserved for his mother. Hers will be the raucous laughter—when she is eighty—that will welcome strangers as she shares photos of her youth and her grandchildren.

She is Cuba.

Ghost #1: The Cars

Haunted Havana

Jonathan A. Taylor

I have a dead friend who lately
Has begun to visit me:
My friend sits down and sings to me,
Sings to me so dolefully…

If his anguish should betray him,
The dead man will curse and weep:
I pat his skull and I lay him,
Lay the dead man down to sleep.

—José Martí, Excerpts from "Poem VIII" of *Versos Sencillos*
Translation by Manuel A. Tellechea

I felt I was in a strange dream, that I'd landed in a world time forgot, that I might be back in the 1950s. A huge blue Chevrolet Bel Air came cruising down the narrow street. The smell of the fumes pouring out with its exhaust mixed with the smell and sight of the accumulated garbage in the street. I tripped on the uneven and broken pavement and remembered I was in Havana—a Havana that, like me, has survived many calamities and seen many ghosts, a

Havana that can be many places and many times where the ghosts of its past present and future—a kind of Scrooge's nightmare—made themselves known.

Ghost #1: The Cars

Although those fumes from the old American cars were definitely real, the cars themselves were mostly ghosts of their former selves. These classic cars were preserved as a matter of necessity, since shortly after Castro came to power in 1959, all car imports were stopped. Soviet mechanical entrails hold together these aging beauties. Many now serve as tourist taxis. Keeping them running is clearly a challenge, as I occasionally saw them off to the side of the road with their hoods open, their owners bent deep inside, tinkering their Frankenstein bodies once again to life. And there are other auto-ghosts, namely the cars of the dead Soviet Union—Ladas, Zils, and Volgas—peppering the Cuban motorways, kept together by consuming each other's parts, qualifying them more as auto zombies, most not long for the road as the harbingers of a new economy—Hyundais, Kias and the occasional ostentatious Mercedes—begin to take over.

Ghost #2: The National Heroes

The next ghosts I encountered were the ghosts of Cuba's national heroes: those spirits that do not change with the amazing upheavals of Cuban culture, that still stick around as remembrances of an idealized past.

José Martí, nineteenth-century poet and political dissident, is a specter I saw all over the city. Many statues are dedicated to him. Passionate in his desire for freedom and equality for all Cubans, Martí dedicated his life to the overthrow of the Spanish rulers oppressing the Cuban people and set the progressive socialist tone for revolutions to come. Cubans clearly love this man they call "the Father of our Country." As one bicycle taxi driver I spoke with explained, "He dedicated this life so we could be here today."

But even I could see that Martí's socialist spirit is waning as Cuba is increasingly being seduced into the free market. Much of Martí's poetry is forgotten, though the ghost of his poetry is still alive in the ever-famous Martí legacy: "Guantanamera" the Cuban folk song based on, among other things, stanzas of Martí's *Versos Sencillos*. As I walked around in Havana, I often heard tourist bands playing "Guantanamera."

I also encountered multiple images of another heroic ghost: Che Guevara. I found Che painted on state buildings, on posters and souvenirs, in state stores and in graffiti all over the city. Founder of the macho idea of the New Cuban Man—the twentieth-century communist macho man who would work for the common good—one would think his idealism and humanitarian ideology would be the main reasons for Che's place in the Cuban pantheon of heroes. However, in talking with many people in Havana, I found that what gives him an almost sacred standing much more secure than that of other revolutionary leaders was his early death fighting in far-off Bolivia. Hermilo, a friend I met in Cuba, told me, "Che was lucky enough to die young. Castro lived longer, long enough to make mistakes. Che never made mistakes; he died a saint."

Che meant to rid Cuba of the vices brought by capitalism: namely the addiction to tourism, gambling and prostitution, and his spirit lingers—the symbol of not just the Revolution but also of an idealist independence.

Of course Fidel Castro's dominant ghost is also present throughout the city. Despite his many imperfections, Fidel is still beloved, especially by the aging adults of the Revolution. Among Millennials, he is held in respect, if not awe. I couldn't go a square block without running into his image somewhere, whether it was an official monument, a picture at a state store, a newspaper clipping or cutout adorning a private business or house. If the Revolution started out glorifying Cuban machismo, it ended glorifying Castro. If Che Guevara fought for a new Cuban culture free of the evils of tourism and prostitution, Castro brought those very two evils back to save the country when Soviet subsidies collapsed with the Berlin wall.

Now, as I walked through Havana I was accosted by an onrush of prostitutes along with the images of Fidel Castro. Tourist attractions are up all over the city. The '50s American cars, once a necessity for travel, have become tourist conveyances. This piecemeal return of the free market economy seems in active revolt against Castro's own socialist revolution. Yet he is the one who was responsible for the introduction of this parallel capitalism, and it may well be a more lasting legacy in Cuba than the ghost of communism.

At El Floridita, a popular bar in Old Havana, I encountered yet another ghost, that of Ernest Hemingway. I found his ghost all over Havana as well, in places like El Floridita, his favorite drinking spot; Hotel Ambos Mundos, his home off and on for nearly eight years; and just outside Havana in a small city called San Francisco de Paula, where Hemingway's former villa, Finca Vigía, still stands. It is at El Floridita that Hemingway sat and sipped his legendary seventeen daiquiris. However, a trip to modern-day El Floridita is not a trip back in time. This bar is hardly the shabby cheap-eats-and-strong-drink joint that Hemingway once enjoyed. Noisy tourist bands play a limited list of old Cuban songs, including the obligatory

"Guantanamera." The bar is actually known for the invention of the daiquiri. It also still serves a special variation of the famous drink made especially for Hemingway called the Papa Doble. One can still order a Papa Doble there, although the drinks are now overpriced and under-rummed. Visitors can also go off to one corner and get their picture taken with a statue of Papa Hemingway. It's reported to be worth the effort since that part of the bar often has the rare wifi signal. Another ghost, it seems. On my trips to the bar, I never got this elusive signal.

It's about a fifteen-minute walk from El Floridita to the Hotel Ambos Mundos where Hemingway lived off and on between 1932-1939. The hotel's room 511 is set aside as the official "Hemingway Room." For the price of five CUCs the curious can visit the faux shrine. The stately hotel is itself a ghost: Sipping a daiquiri on this roof terrace I could easily imagine Papa Hemingway's ghost leisurely taking in the beautiful views of Havana, drink in hand.

Another Hemingway haunt near Havana is his former villa, Finca Vigía. There, the official tour guide was quick to tout a picture of Hemingway with Fidel Castro, mentioning that Hemingway was a strong supporter of the Revolution. The tour guide claimed that Hemingway donated his villa to the cause. There is some debate about this. In the end, the books and the villa remain a museum where the only thing they gather is dust.

Ghost #3: Our Shadows

The history of Havana's Vedado district, or the Forbidden area, is that the Spanish called it "forbidden" as a way to keep rebels away from the city of Havana. Even today all sorts of forbidden activities take place in the Vedado. Of all the illicit activities, none is quite so close to my heart as the rather shadowy yet trendy LGBT scene.

Cuba is not a society where homosexuality has gained a legitimate presence. Just like other specters in Havana, the LGBT community is tolerated but unofficial. Havana's cool tolerance is also quite recent, dating to the coming out of Raúl Castro's daughter, Mariela Castro. Apparently as late as 2015, it was still acceptable for the police to round up gay men hanging out at certain meeting points. I'm told they would be jailed and forced to clean the police station before they could go home. Having said that, the gay community is cautiously getting a shadow of a presence. At a Vedado restaurant, aptly named Toke, there are two gay flags in the back of the bar, scarcely noticeable from the outside terrace where a couple friends—Hermilo and Florian—and I ate a Cuban take on spaghetti pomodoro. My friend Hermilo, a tall former model, and I marveled at the homemade gay flags in the restaurant.

"Don't get too excited, sweetie," Hermilo intoned with his elegant, effeminate voice. "Hardly anyone in Cuba besides us even knows what that flag means."

Later that night, we rendezvoused at the Malecón. The Malecón is the meeting spot where Havanans hang out in the open air. There is a gay section, but it was too noisy and distracting for my friends. Instead we went a little further down to a spot where we were more isolated. Hermilo played his secret stash of house music on a portable radio. In a short time, we were surrounded by teenage boys who had gathered to dance to Hermilo's music with their girlfriends. Another friend brought a bottle of rum. Someone else bought bags of popcorn from an enterprising old lady who sold them from a basket.

Afterwards, we went to a small trendy club. The crowd was not particularly gay, but was clearly gay-friendly. Everyone was looking very chic. The club is housed in a Moorish-Spanish hall where almost all the decor has been removed except for industrial seating along a bar and some benches on the rooftop. Florian, Hermilo and I ascended to the roof where we heard music and dancing. As the beautiful people wrapped in their beautiful CUC-paid clothes mingled and chatted, Florian and I sat on a bench. We looked at each other and he grew quiet.

"I wonder if it is okay to kiss you here?" he mused.

I looked around to see the self-absorbed throng cramming into each other.

"I don't think anyone will notice." I said. The next thing I knew, Florian's tongue was down my throat.

I was right. Nobody noticed.

A Ghostly Goodbye:

Of course Havana has many other ghosts: the Revolution, ration books and Communism among them. My closing ghost, however, is phone service. On my way to the airport I finally got some mobile telephone reception. As a trickle of emails downloaded, I decided to send Florian and Hermilo a last farewell. I quickly typed out a message, hit the send button, got the magical send message, and then just as quickly this notification: "Messages to this country code are not supported."

And there it was: my final farewell thwarted by yet another ghost—the ghost of a broken U.S. relationship, a spirit I neglected to cover in my ghostly Havana catalog.

Recipe for a Papa Doble

Two ounces Havana Club three-year-old rum
½ ounce freshly squeezed grapefruit juice
½ ounce freshly squeezed lime juice
¼ ounce maraschino liqueur
One to two tbsp sugar (optional)
Shaved ice

Mix rum, grapefruit juice, lime juice, sugar and maraschino liquor over ice. Strain and pour over shaved ice. A more traditional version would be poured over crushed ice.

Step into the journey, Poet ...

Poet

Linda Watanabe McFerrin

For Thanasis, November 18, 2017

This is your journey, Poet,
the one you know you must take.
You have put it off for too long
while you traveled the world—
the world you loved like a woman,
the women you loved like the world.

Now it is upon you.
Your sails are full,
though you long one more time
to feel the cobbles,
the grass beneath your feet,
the tree bark under your hands.

You must turn your back on Cuba, on Greece,
on the byways and roads that still call you
to beautiful stories and poems.
A New World awaits.
Old friends beckon.
Step into the journey, Poet.

Now you are the story; you are the poem.

Street art at a construction site in Old Havana

Glossary

Special Period	extended period of economic crisis in Cuba beginning in 1989 with dissolution of the Soviet Union and Comecon (The Council for Mutual Economic Assistance).
CUC	Cuban convertible peso
peso	the currency in Cuba reserved for local use
casa particular	private house or homestay in Cuba
paladar	restaurant run by self-employers
Santería	pantheistic Afro-Cuban religion
finca	country estate or ranch
danzón	official music genre and dance of Cuba
bollito	Mexican version of French bread also common in Cuba
sala	living room

Band in a public area of downtown Havana

Author Biographies

A former high-tech executive, **Tania Romanov Amochaev** is a writer, traveler and award-winning photographer. She was born in Serbia and has lived most of her life in San Francisco. Writing as Tania Romanov, her book, *Mother Tongue: A Saga of Three Generations of Balkan Women*, tells of exile and separation amid the unrelenting consequences of 100 years of Balkan wars. Tania's work has been published in *Best Travel Writing* Volumes 10 and 11, *Hidden Compass, The Dickens,* and *Wandering in Andalusia*. *My First Trip to the Homeland, Book One of Travels With Tania*, is available on Kindle and other e-book platforms.

Adrienne Amundsen is a psychologist, specializing in trauma, grief, and creativity. Born in Texas, but long ago transplanted to Northern California, she is the mother of two grown boys. Her poetry has been published in a number of literary journals and anthologies, and her first poetry collection, *Cassandras Falling*, was published in 2011. Dr. Amundsen's interests have taken her from the caves of France to the war zone in Afghanistan, and she has taught classes on shamanism and cave art both locally in California and internationally. She works with a local nonprofit organization, Afghans 4 Tomorrow, which helps Afghans provide girls' education and economic opportunities for families. Her second poetry collection, *Reclaiming the Apple*, was published in 2014.

Christine Berardo left a rewarding career writing movies and miniseries for television to work on a novel in Northern California where the roots to her writing began. She's been writing poems, stories, song lyrics and journals since childhood. Her poems and a short story were recently published in the Redwood Writers anthologies *Stolen Light* and *Sonoma Stories*. A native of San Francisco, Chris has lived in Los Angeles, Washington, D.C., Palo Alto and London. Work in film and television took her to far-flung parts of the world: Warsaw, Sydney, Manila, Cape Town, Halifax and Budapest, among others. Over the years she's worn other hats, including public school teacher, piano teacher, political activist, community volunteer, wife, mother, grandmother. She now lives in Healdsburg with her husband and their collie, Homer.

Sandra Bracken made the first of many journeys alone to Peru where she walked the hills around Sacsayhuaman, photographed the stonework there and chartered a plane to fly over the lines at Nazca—all in the pursuit of art. She has a Master's Degree in Fine Arts, taught drawing for twenty years and has exhibited sculpture and drawings in galleries and museums in the U.S. She collaborated on a collection of poems and collages, *Meet Me at the Wayside Body Shop*, and produced a chapbook of poems, *New Moon*.

Her travel stories were included in *Venturing in Ireland: Quest for the Modern Celtic Soul; Venturing in Italy: Puglia, Land between Two Seas; Wandering in Paris: Luminaries and Love in the City of Light; Wandering in Cornwall: Mystery, Mirth and Transformation in the Land of Ancient Celts* and *Wandering in Andalusia: The Soul of Southern Spain*. She lives in Maryland near her three children and five grandchildren. Her most recent travels have been with her husband—in pursuit of fish.

Cyndi Goddard grew up under the pale sky of Florida's west coast. She studied creative writing at Tulane University in New Orleans and Spanish art and literature in Madrid. After college, Cyndi spent six months exploring Paris and writing her first novel. This book, along with her backpack, disappeared on a Greyhound journey from New York City to Texas.

After alighting briefly in Austin, then Los Angeles, Cyndi made her home in San Francisco's Mission District, where she composed lyrics for a punk band, and poetry and short fiction for small literary magazines. She lived with her husband on a sailboat on San Francisco Bay for ten years. During that time, they had two children and cruised the coasts of California and Mexico, adventures that Cyndi chronicled in magazines such as *Sail, Cruising World, Sailing, Latitude 38* and regional sailing publications. Cyndi was selected to participate in both the Squaw Valley and the Writers Hotel Conferences. She is a member of Sisters in Crime and Left Coast Writers. Her current writing projects are a mystery novel and the first volume of a near-future science fiction series.

Douglas Hale is a senior economist retired after thirty-four fun-filled years in the Department of Defense (Systems Analysis), the Environmental Protection Agency (Program Planning and Analysis) and the Department of Energy (Energy Information Administration). The vast majority of his writings have such compelling titles as *Nonparametric Comparative Statics and Stability* (Princeton University

Press), *Buying Time: Franchising Hazardous and Nuclear Waste Cleanup* (the *Energy Journal*) and *Derivatives and Risk Management in the Petroleum, Natural Gas, and Electricity Industries* (EIA). Now living in the Oakland Hills, far from Washington D.C., he is busy enjoying life and hoping that readers will find "¿Viva la Revolución?" as riveting as his early classics.

Thomas Harrell has joined the ranks of former lawyers who became writers. After sixteen years working for a Wall Street firm, the last six on dialysis, he received a new kidney eight years ago. With this second chance, he decided to leave the law and pursue two of his life passions: travel and writing. He has traveled to numerous countries, although not nearly enough yet. He has written about travel in several of these countries, including Argentina, Bosnia, China and Italy. A frequent contributor to the Wanderland anthology series, Tom also writes personal essays, many set in the South, where he was raised. He studied history and politics in college and is writing a spy novel set during the Civil War. He lives in San Francisco, California.

Donna Hemmila finds the best travel experiences arise from her inability to understand maps, even the electronic kind that talks to you. She inevitably turns left down narrow passageways when she should have gone straight. At those times, she thinks of her grandmother, Sophie, who left Poland at the age of twenty-two, bound for America with nine dollars in her pocket and a desire only to see what was waiting around the next bend. Hint: It will always be something amazing you didn't expect. Donna has worked as a news reporter, business editor, and speechwriter and was a contributor to *Wandering in Andalusia: The Soul of Southern Spain*. She lives in Berkeley, California, and writes children's books.

Author Biographies

Linda Jue was inspired by Watergate to become an investigative reporter more than forty years ago. Since then, she has uncovered international political intrigue behind a local murder, exposed the politics of homelessness in San Francisco, documented the trends of Asian organized crime and tracked down the fates of fleeing dissidents after Tiananmen Square. She was also a co-founder and senior advisor of a historic and multiple award-winning collaboration between several dozen Bay Area and national media organizations to investigate the murder of a journalist in Oakland, California. She has won several journalism awards.

Currently, Linda is an editor-at-large for 100Reporters, a national investigative reporting news site based in Washington, D.C. She also works as a consultant to media and community organizations to improve investigative reporting practices as well as diversify journalism's ranks. She is past president of the Northern California Chapter of the Society of Professional Journalists, during which she led the chapter in precedent-setting journalism initiatives that inspired changes in practices in journalism nationwide.

Linda is a former associate of the Center for Investigative Reporting and a former editor at *San Francisco Focus* magazine/KQED. Her work has appeared in *San Francisco Focus*, the *San Francisco Bay Guardian*, *SF Weekly*, *GEO*, *Consumer Health Interactive*, *Los Angeles Times* Syndicate, *Toronto Globe and Mail*, the *MacNeil/Lehrer NewsHour*, PBS' *Frontline*, and other outlets. She also worked as the Northern California correspondent for C-SPAN.

Carol J. Kelly was born in Jamaica and moved to the United States after graduating high school. She considers herself bicultural, seeing the world through the lens of a Caribbean native and as a U.S. citizen and longtime New Yorker. She has extensive experience as a copy editor, news editor and staff writer at top companies, including the *Boston Globe* and the *Wall Street Journal*. She was part of an editing team that helped the *Journal* win a Pulitzer Prize for its 9/11 coverage. Her profile of a deaf basketball player who represented the U.S. at an international sporting event won an NYABJ award for best feature story (Community Newspapers). Carol has been published across media platforms, and has co-edited a number of anthologies of personal essays written by and for teenagers.

Carol contributed her own travel essays to *Venturing in Italy: Travels in Puglia, Land between Two Seas*. Cuba is one of her special places of the heart—she's besotted with the island's music, its culture, and its people. She is also passionate about tennis and photography. Carol lives in Brooklyn, New York, where she's working on a family memoir that examines the experience of being left behind in Jamaica when her mother migrated to England.

Laurie McAndish King loves peering through the looking glass. She has published two collections of stories: *Lost, Kidnapped, Eaten Alive! True Stories from a Curious Traveler,* and *Your Crocodile has Arrived: More True Stories from a Curious Traveler*. Her essays and photography have appeared in *Smithsonian* magazine, Lonely Planet, the *San Francisco Chronicle*, Travelers' Tales' *Best Women's Travel Writing*, and other magazines and literary anthologies. They have also garnered many awards, including the Lowell Thomas Gold Award, bestowed by the American Society of Travel Writers, and a First Place in Photography award from the Smithsonian.

Laurie also wrote *An Erotic Alphabet* and co-edited, along with Linda Watanabe McFerrin, two volumes of erotica in the *Hot Flashes: Sexy little stories and poems* series. She has an undergraduate degree in philosophy and a master's degree in education, and enjoys gardening and taxidermy. LaurieMcAndishKing.com

Author Biographies

As a boy growing up in Brooklyn, **Robert Markowitz** set out to be a writer. He went to Boston University to pursue that dream. But after that he got sidetracked by life. First as a print journalist (AP, UP). Then as a documentary filmmaker (CBS News). Ten years later he woke up in a Hollywood dream factory and discovered that he had been kidnapped and seduced into becoming a director of movies and miniseries for television. He never stopped writing. He wrote what William Saroyan called his "unwritten, written novels." After years of plotting, he escaped to Northern California where he is happily writing his first novel, T*he Lost Boy*.

Mary Jean Pramik, a coalminer's daughter and a great, great-granddaughter of the Mongolian plain, has hitch-hiked across the United States, tracked May Apples in Ohio, chased children through wet mountains of California, fended off bill collectors in tropical San Francisco, and counted sharp-talon bird carcasses along the Pacific's Point Reyes sands. Communicating with screeching penguin hoards in Antarctica remains a high point of her sojourn on this planet.

MJ earned undergraduate and graduate degrees in biological sciences, and completed an MFA in Writing. She moonlights as a medical writer, penning such scientific thrillers as *Norenthindrone, The First Three Decades*, the fast-paced history of the first birth control pill extracted from a Mexican yam. Winner of the coveted Mary Womer Medal and a Travelers' Tales Solas Award, MJ's articles and essays have appeared in *Nature Biotechnology, Drug Topics,* and *Cosmetic Surgery News,* and mainstream publications such as *Good Housekeeping, Odyssey,* and the *National Enquirer*. She has contributed to the "*Venturing in*" travel series on the Canal du Midi, Southern Greece, Southern Ireland, and Puglia, Italy. MJ teaches graduate writing skills in the College of Science and Engineering at San Francisco State University.

Anne Sigmon flunked jump rope in seventh grade and washed out of college P.E. After college, she headed for San Francisco and a career in public relations. Exotic travel was the stuff of dreams until, at thirty-eight, she married Jack, took tea with erstwhile headhunters in Borneo and climbed Mt. Kilimanjaro at forty-three. Five years later, she was zapped by a career-ending stroke caused by an obscure autoimmune disease called Antiphospholipid Syndrome (APS). She may be stuck with blood thinners and a damaged brain, but she's still traveling to isolated regions ranging from Botswana to Burma and, most recently, to Syria, Jordan and a remote rainforest in Costa Rica.

Anne's personal essays and travel stories have appeared in local and national publications including *Good Housekeeping* and *Stroke Connection* magazines and the anthologies *Wandering in Costa Rica, Chicken Soup for the Soul: Find Your Happiness* and *Travel Stories from Around the Globe.* She is currently working on a memoir about her experience with stroke and autoimmune disease. Anne's blog, JunglePants.com, offers travel tales and tips about adventure travel off the beaten path. On Anne's author website (annesigmon.com), she writes about—and offers tips on—living with stroke and autoimmune disease.

Jonathan A. Taylor is a San Francisco-based writer and designer. He is a leading designer for creating user-friendly technology and has worked for companies such as Google, Nokia, IBM, and GE, as well as for the Dutch design bureaus Informaat and Stroomt Interactions. Jonathan has published two books on software design.

Jonathan's passions include theater, opera, travel, social justice and cooking. All of these passions figure prominently in his writing. A leader in the community of alternative sexuality, he is the title-holder of the 2013 International Master/Slave Education title, which he earned with his now deceased husband Morris Taylor. Jonathan's novel, *The Rites of Passage*, is the first installment of a multi-volume series, *The Goldberg Variations*, which are his first works of fiction.

Anne Woods is a commercial pilot and flight instructor. A third generation pilot, she soloed a glider on her fourteenth birthday. She has a Bachelor of Arts in English from the University of the Pacific. Her short story, "Riding the Wave," was a finalist in the 2011 William Faulkner-William Wisdom Creative Writing Competition. Her articles have appeared in *Pacific Flyer* and *In Flight* magazine. Two of her travel essays were published in *Venturing in Southern Greece: The Vatika Odysseys*. Anne is writing a non-fiction book about World War II fighter pilot James L. Brooks. She lives in the San Francisco Bay Area.

Editor Biographies

Joanna Biggar is a teacher, writer and traveler whose special places of the heart include the California coast and the south of France. She has degrees in Chinese and French and, as a professional writer for thirty years, has written poetry, fiction, personal essays, features, news and travel articles for hundreds of publications including *The Washington Post Magazine*, *Psychology Today*, the *International Herald Tribune* and the *Wall Street Journal*. Her book *Travels and Other Poems* was published in 1996, and her most recent travel essays have appeared in the Wandering series, whose anthologies include books on Costa Rica, Bali, Paris, Cornwall and Andalusia. *That Paris Year*, the first in a trilogy published by Alan Squire Publishing in 2010 will be followed by the second, *Melanie's Song*, in 2019.

She has taught journalism, creative writing, personal essay and travel writing in many venues, and has juried the annual awards for the Northern California chapter of the Society of Professional Journalists. She serves on the Board of Directors of Emiliano Zapata Street Academy in Oakland, California, where she makes her home, and is a longtime member of the Society of Woman Geographers. More information is on her blog, www.joannabiggar.org.

Editor Biographies

Linda Watanabe McFerrin (www.lwmcferrin.com) is a poet, travel writer, novelist and contributor to numerous newspapers, magazines and anthologies. She is the author of two poetry collections, past editor of a popular Northern California guidebook and a winner of the Katherine Anne Porter Prize for Fiction. Her novel, *Namako: Sea Cucumber,* was named Best Book for the Teen-Age by the New York Public Library. In addition to authoring an award-winning short story collection, *The Hand of Buddha,* she has co-edited twelve anthologies, including the *Hot Flashes: sexy little stories & poems* series. Her latest novel, *Dead Love* (Stone Bridge Press, 2009), was a Bram Stoker Award Finalist for Superior Achievement in a Novel.

Linda has judged the San Francisco Literary Awards, the Josephine Miles Award for Literary Excellence and the Kiriyama Prize, served as a visiting mentor for the Loft Mentor Series and been guest faculty at the Oklahoma Arts Institute. A past NEA Panelist and juror for the Marin Literary Arts Council and the founder of Left Coast Writers®, she has led workshops in Greece, France, Italy, England, Ireland, Central America, Indonesia, Spain and the United States and has mentored a long list of accomplished writers and best-selling authors toward publication.

A collection of Linda's selected works is forthcoming from Alan Squire Publishing in 2019.

www.ingramcontent.com/pod-product-compliance
Lightning Source LLC
Chambersburg PA
CBHW052020070526
44584CB00016B/1840